ART
Basic for Young Children

Lila Lasky and Rose Mukerji-Bergeson

The National Association for the Education of Young Children
Washington, D.C.

Cover art: Jean McCann (at age six)

Design and Figures 7-9, 11-15, and 17-22: Caroline Taylor

Figures 10 and 16: Rebecca Miller

Photos: Susie Fitzhugh x; Elaine M. Ward 19, 41, 76, 84, 109, 113, 130, 136; Judy Burr 20; Faith Bowlus 23, 110; Marietta Lynch 32, 68; Rose Engel 47; Mr. and Mrs. Guy L. Robbins 53; Sandy Felsenthal 55; Michael D. Sullivan 57, 119; Betty C. Ford 58; Mary K. Gallagher 66; Toge Fujihira 71; Melvin Suhd 74; Elisabeth Nichols 87; Michael McCoy 88; Joel Freeman 98; Jean Berlfein 114; Lois Main 125; Clyde Mueller 128

Second printing 1982, third printing 1984, fourth printing 1987, fifth printing 1990, sixth printing 1992, seventh printing 1995, eighth printing 2001.

National Association for the Education of Young Children
1509 16th Street, NW
Washington, DC 20036-1426
202-232-8777 or 800-424-2460
www.naeyc.org

Through its publications program the National Association for the Education of Young Children (NAEYC) provides a forum for discussion of major issues and ideas in the early childhood field, with the hope of provoking thought and promoting professional growth. The views expressed or implied are not necessarily those of the Association. NAEYC wihes to thank the authors, who donated much time and effort to develop this book for the profession.

Library of Congress Catalog Card Number: 80-82565
ISBN Catalog Number: 0-912674-73-3
NAEYC #106

Printed in the United States of America

To Jerry and Prafulla and young Scott

Contents

Preface

Young children are passionate learners. From infancy, they marshall an incredible amount of energy in developing. In their early years, children build an ever-expanding web of living in a world of people, events, and things. The thrust of their growth and development strengthens their distinctive personality. Adults, who have their own personality networks, enter the child's web of life at many points. This book emphasizes those contacts which support young children's capacity to develop and learn through art.

As caring adults, we must continually deepen our understanding of growing children to nurture them effectively as they gain strength for coping with the world. In addition, we must enrich our knowledge of the specific content around which fruitful relationships develop. Art is one of many dynamic forces that strengthen the young child's personality.

In our many years of teaching young children from nursery through the primary grades, we have learned not only *about* children, but also *from* children. We have seriously reflected on the creative process and how the arts can enhance development and learning in young children. We have spent years working with prospective and practicing early childhood teachers while always remaining in touch with young children. We now want to share what we have learned, and are still learning, about why and how art is basic in young children's lives.

This book reflects our view that the growing, learning child is central to early childhood education and that art is an especially beautiful pathway toward development. Therefore, Chapter 4 provides extensive practical detail about art for young children. Other chapters focus on a more comprehensive view of children learning in art and other curriculum areas. Based on his extensive study of children and their drawings, Dr. Joseph Di Leo, author of Chapter 2, shares his findings about child development and creativity as they relate to art. We are indebted to him for his significant contribution to this book.

We invite you to share our thinking about the importance of art in the education of young children and our conviction that art is basic to the quality of their lives.

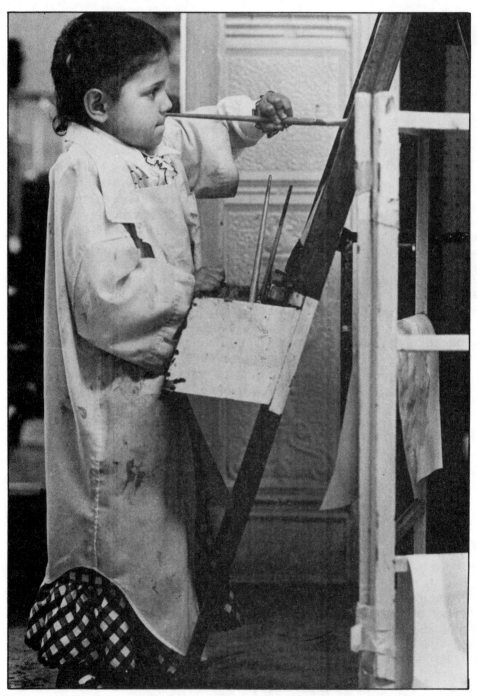

If we relegate learning through art to second-class status and treat it as a frill, then we shortchange children.

1
Young Children Need Art

Are we shortchanging children? Do we expand or limit children's natural zest for dealing with the world? If we carefully examine art programs for two- to eight-year-old children, we will have substantial information for answering these questions.

Young children make phenomenal strides in growth and development in their early years. They have learned to walk, run, climb, and successfully get around on their own before they come to schools or child care centers. They also have figured out how to talk the same language as the people around them, have developed ideas based on their encounters with the world, and have voracious appetites for knowing and doing.

Anyone watching young children in these early years sees the results of integrated learning. Young children actively use sound, sight, touch, smell, and taste to form perceptions, organize simple patterns, and sense relationships.

Integrated learning is natural, but it will not occur automatically without conscious contributions from adults. What *kind* of guidance do we give young children at home, in schools, and in children's centers? Do we support children's broad interests and many-faceted ways of knowing? Or do we constrict children by overemphasizing such tasks as labeling colors, shapes, numerals, and letters at the expense of a more balanced education?

If we relegate learning through art to second-class status and treat it as a frill, then we shortchange children. If, however, we treat art as basic to education, then we are in accord with philosophers as far back as Plato, who believed in humanism and the good life through comprehensive education. Contemporary voices continue to speak eloquently about the importance of art in education.

Art is basic education

The Arts, Education and Americans Panel, chaired by David Rockefeller, Jr., stated,

This Panel supports the concept of "basic education," but maintains that the arts, properly taught, are basic to individual development since they, more than any other subject, awaken all the senses—the learning pores. We endorse a curriculum which puts "basics"

1

first, because the arts are basic, right at the heart of the matter. And we suggest not that reading be replaced by art but that the concept of literacy be expanded beyond word skills. (American Council for the Arts in Education 1977, p. 6)

We strongly agree with the Panel. Art must be acknowledged as basic to individual development and must, therefore, be taught effectively beginning in the early years. A growing number of schools realize that an art program is not only for the talented. "The new arts education recognizes that the arts *are* basic education. They represent fundamental ways of knowing (Fowler 1976, p. 72)."

Such fundamental learning is demonstrated by a group of six-year-old children interested in a planting activity. In preparation for the annual school-wide garden project, many of the first-grade children were planting seeds. Several children had selected lima beans, which were initially planted on blotters in see-through plastic cups so that children might better observe the germination and growth process. The children recorded the changing events in a scientist's log, and made their own drawings of the growth process. Then they put the drawings together to make a simulated movie. This faithful recording of lima bean progress clarified the children's perceptions of the growth process. The changes in the beans and the roots were carefully represented in succeeding pictures. Through this activity, with its natural melding of science and art, the children sharpened their sensory awareness and formed more accurate concepts of growth and change in nature.

This simple project also provided children with other important learnings. Problem solving and discipline were integral parts of making a movie about limas. A strong cardboard box was converted into a frame for the screen. As the reel-to-reel system was effectively translated into a roller-to-roller system, the children learned how certain machines work. Mathematical skills were strengthened by standardizing the size of each picture to the size of the screen opening. The long roll of shelf paper was now ready for drawings of the horizontal pictures as the beans developed.

An unexpected question of the discipline inherent in art arose at one point. Concentrating on the elongated roots and slender, tall stem, Kevin drew his picture vertically. It did not fit the limits of the horizontal frame, and he could not trim it without losing part of the plant growth. He objected to turning the picture on its side because "That's not the way it grows." The limits of the art form required that he make his picture horizontal while still retaining the integrity of his perception. Kevin made a new picture that fit, and the original was saved to illustrate a dictated story of why it could not be used in the movie.

This one example of a typical curriculum activity for young children demonstrates how the art activity helped sharpen perceptual awareness; supported a beginning concept of growth and change in life; engaged children in the use of math and physics in solving a self-selected, real problem; and helped them accept the necessary discipline for a successful group project. The example affirmed that art *is* basic education. Perhaps these children will someday understand Read's statement: "In the end I do not distinguish science and art, except as methods. . . . Art is the representation, science the explanation—of the same reality (Read 1974, p. 11)."

Art is a distinctive way of knowing

Art is both a fundamental and distinctive way of knowing. According to Houston, "A person needs to think in terms of images as well as words (Read 1974, p. 11)."

Current research (Languis, Sanders, and Tipps 1980) shows how the left and right hemispheres in the brain control distinctive ways of knowing. "The left hemisphere [of the brain] 'specializes' in data . . . built across time . . . [needed in reading and listening]; the right hemisphere 'specializes' in data . . . built across space . . . [and] has been called the visual-spatial brain (Hunter 1976, p. 45)." Who can minimize the importance of what children learn through seeing their three-dimensional world? Who can fail to appreciate the value of an art program to visual-spatial learning and to developing the powers of the right hemisphere of the growing child's brain?

An effective art program can do even more:

> Our personal development is based on what happens to us in the two worlds in which we live. One is the external physical world of things and events; the other is the inner world of senses, feelings and meanings. Art activities are important because they form a bridge of communication and interaction between these two worlds. (Czurles 1977, p. 5)

Children's art is also important as a nonverbal language, a system of symbols emerging from children's early scribbling (Francks 1979). Children can communicate thoughts and feelings in art before they develop more conventional means of expressing ideas and emotions in words. Although children's art symbols may not always be recognized or understood by adults, those children who are given opportunities to engage in expressive art use symbols that assist them in creating meaning for themselves about their world.

A mixed-age class of four- to six-year-old children was captivated while waiting for incubating eggs to hatch. The group's excitement increased as the zero hour approached, and the children eagerly awaited the tapping sounds that would signal the eventful cracking of the shells.

Cindy, the youngest child, wore a path between the easel and the incubator. At the easel, she was dabbing small yellow strokes all over the paper. With the first feeble tapping of the chicks against the shells, she began dabbing red strokes all over the paper. Finally, one shell cracked open. Cindy rushed to the easel, and painted a bold, dramatic line the whole length of her picture.

Anyone seeing the picture in isolation would not understand its meaning. But by watching Cindy paint, it was clear her growing sense of expectation and urgency was expressed in paint rather than in words. Her exultant "crack!" as she finished the red streak confirmed that the painting was her effective, and primarily nonverbal, means of dealing with a powerful emotion—the birth of new life.

Education through art

When we value art as basic education and as a distinctive way of knowing, we can appreciate the importance for children of education through art. The following values of art will be discussed throughout this book.

When young children engage in expressive art activities they—
- can give vent to thoughts and emotions in healthy, growth-producing ways;
- gain a sense of accomplishment which helps move them along the path toward self-affirmation;
- dare to try new ways of doing things;
- develop the ability to make choices;
- grow toward achieving independence and autonomy;
- appreciate the value of tools in human hands;
- learn about the properties of a variety of materials;
- begin to accept and value the work of others as well as their own;
- heighten their perceptual powers;
- grow to meet new challenges with greater flexibility;
- come to appreciate the aesthetic elements in their environment.

In summarizing the significance of the arts for American education, the Arts, Education and Americans Panel stated convincingly that

. . . learning *in* the arts is of unique educational value . . . learning *about* the arts is learning about the rich world of sensation, emotion, and personal expression surrounding us each day . . . learning *through* the arts has the potential to enhance one's general motivation to learn and to develop one's respect for a disciplined approach to learning. (American Council for the Arts in Education 1977, p. 8)

References

American Council for the Arts in Education. *Coming to Our Senses: The Significance of the Arts for American Education.* New York: McGraw-Hill, 1977.

Czurles, S. A. "Art and the Ten Goals for Elementary, Secondary, and Continuing Education." New York State Art Teachers Association, North Syracuse, N.Y., 1977.

Fowler, C. B. "The New Arts Education." *Today's Education* 65, no. 2 (March-April 1976): 72-74.

Francks, O. R. "Scribbles? Yes, They *Are* Art!" *Young Children* 34, no. 5 (July 1979): 14-22.

Hunter, M. "Right-Brained Kids in Left-Brained Schools." *Today's Education* 65, no. 4 (November-December 1976): 45-48.

Languis, M.; Sanders, T.; and Tipps, S. *Brain and Learning: Directions in Early Childhood Education.* Washington, D.C.: National Association for the Education of Young Children, 1980.

Read, H. *Education Through Art.* New York: Pantheon, 1974.

Williams, R. M. "Why Children Should Draw: The Surprising Link Between Art and Learning." *Saturday Review* 4, no. 23 (September 3, 1977): 11-16.

2

Graphic Activity of Young Children: Development and Creativity

Joseph H. Di Leo, M.D.
Director, Developmental Clinic
New York Foundling Hospital 1945-1978
Lecturer, Department of Special Education
Teachers College, Columbia University

> Art activity cannot be imposed but must come as a spirit from within. This is not always an easy process, but the development of creative abilities is essential in our society, and the youngster's drawing reflects his creative growth both in the drawing itself and in the process of making the art form. (Lowenfeld and Brittain 1975)

Today, perhaps more effectively and more efficiently than at any other time, an outside force—the machine—determines the pattern of our lives. If we are to retain our dignity and the freedom to think and feel independently, a bulwark will have to be erected against the conformism inherent in technological suppression of the human spirit. With the contemporary decline of family influence, the task falls increasingly upon education in the schools. The expressive arts remain a potent force against the aridity of an all-pervasive technology. Because of their universal appeal, the arts may well assume a central position around which other disciplines can be structured. Early participation in the visual arts can sustain the flame of creative self-expression present in every young child (Read 1973).

This chapter examines the graphic activity of young children and its relationship to creativity and development. Creativity may be broadly applied to any activity that results in something that was not there before. In that sense, children's early kinesthetic scribblings may be regarded as a creation. In a more restricted sense, the term may be more properly applied to the mental process that directs the child's eye and hand to arrange lines and circles in the symbolic representation of a person, animal, or object. In most children, this level of creativity is attained sometime between the ages of three and four years. The essence of creativity lies in the approach which the individual child brings to the solution of a problem—in this instance, the symbolic representation of the subject. Individuality accounts for the differences in drawings at comparable stages of development, which are similar but not identical.

Direct observation of young children supports the belief that they are endowed with the urge, capacity, and need to be creative. In all cultures, and probably in all times, human beings have left a visual record of their interests, desires, and fears in caves and on walls, from the marvelous imagery of Altamira and Laxcaux to the graffiti of Pompeii. Today, as in the past, children delight in scribbling and drawing. The universality of the behavior and the uniformity of sequences in the development of concepts (Piaget 1955) and in their graphic expression (Luquet 1913) bear striking testimony to the essential unity of humanity.

The earliest available children's drawings appear in a small volume by Corrado Ricci (1887). Undoubtedly, children had been drawing long before that time, but apparently no one took them seriously. It is only during the past hundred years that children's drawings have been studied and preserved. Following the publication of Ricci's book, reproductions of children's drawings appeared in other countries. Notable are publications by Levinstein (1905), Claparède (1946), Rouma (1919), Goodenough (1926), Eng (1954), Kellogg (1967), Harris (1963), and Lansing (1969).

Children have been seen as persons in their own right and not merely as diminutive or defective adults only during the past hundred years. Graphic activity has been recognized as a manifestation of the thoughts and feelings proper to developing children, whose drawings change and grow along with the children. Essentially unaffected by time and space, drawings of the past century show the same progressions and peculiarities as those by contemporary children everywhere.

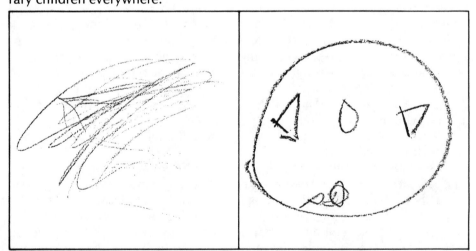

Fig. 1. Zigzag drawing (27-month-old boy).   Fig. 2. Drawing of a person (four-year-old child).

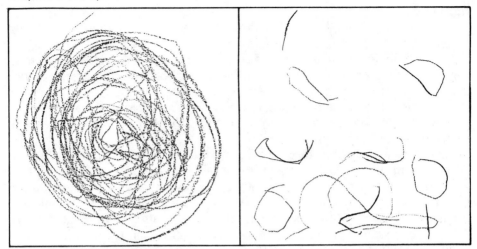

Fig. 3. Continuous whorl (32-month-old girl).   Fig. 4. Discrete circles (38-month-old girl).

Stages of development

Drawings by young children may be divided into two broad groupings: an early scribbling or kinesthetic phase which begins at about 15 months, and a later representational phase which begins sometime between 3 and 4 years of age.

The earliest scribblings are likely to be zigzag (Figure 1). These evolve into a variety of configurations as children develop better control. By about age three, children make circles that become the salient feature of their drawings. Even this early phase is not devoid of significance. The secure, well-adjusted child will happily scribble freely across the available space. In contrast, the insecure child will make timid, barely visible, broken strokes in the lower corner of the paper.

The next broad category, representational drawing, is evident at age four and henceforth dominates children's art. Representational drawing is a deliberate symbolic attempt to represent graphically an animate or inanimate object in the child's environment (Figure 2).

Between these two broad groupings, there is the thrilling and unexpected discovery that the casually scribbled circle could intentionally be made to represent something important, possibly a head. This "quantum jump" opens the way to representational drawing. Children will occasionally slide back into scribbling, but the direction of growth is like a spiral that winds up and down, always a bit higher and a little less lower, so that representational drawing is bound to dominate. The drawings will be progressively more recognizable and complex. The favorite subject is likely to be the one most significant in the child's life—people. The human figure is by far the favorite subject of all young artists.

Many investigators have described the invariant sequences through which the human figure evolves, but Luquet (1913) has interpreted their meaning most clearly.

The first stage, which Luquet called "le dessin involontaire," is nonrepresentational. Children derive pleasure from the movement and from watching the movement leave its record on a surface. The early zigzag becomes more regular as children gain better control over scribbling. Circular movements prevail at about three years of age. At first the configurations are in the form of a continuous whorl or skein (Figure 3). Children's expressions reveal the delight with which they watch the crayon go 'round and 'round while the figure grows with each additional coil.

Later, the circles will be discrete (Figure 4). One of them will suggest a head. At this point, the child has made a first graphic symbol and is then at the threshold of the next stage: representational drawing. This first stage of representation will be characterized by what Luquet has termed "intellectual realism" because children draw what they know rather than what they see. Their drawings are representations, not reproductions, and the result is expressionistic, not impressionistic.

To the primordial circle will soon be added two smaller ones to represent the eyes. The earliest additions to the oversized head and face will be the four limbs represented by four lines issuing from the head (Figure 5). This figure has been observed throughout the world, wherever the drawings have been given serious attention. In the English-speaking world it is called a *tadpole* or *cephalopod;* in Germany, *kopffüssler;* in France, *bonhomme tétard;* in Italy, *omino testone;* in Spanish-language countries, *renacuajo.*

Ricci saw and reproduced such figures more than a century ago (1887) and today we see the same tadpoles by four- and five-year-old children. Eventually, a small body will be added, often adorned with the fascinating, mysterious belly button (Figure 6). In time, other features will express the child's progressive maturation.

Another peculiarity is children's insistence on portraying what is known to exist (Luquet's intellectual realism). In complete disregard of whether the person or object can actually be seen, but knowing that there is a man in the bell tower pulling the rope, the child will show him clearly through the stone wall. People in a boat will be seen through the hull. Both legs of the woman astride a horse will be shown. This "X-ray technique" is typically seen before age seven. But even later at about age nine, when many children begin to prefer drawing profiles, the tendency to include what is known may impel the addition of a second eye and then a second nose between the two eyes.

This amusing feature, perfectly understandable as a transitional uncertainty between full-face and profile rendition, would be grossly abnormal were it to be an expression of profile confusion in an adolescent. Normal at one age, such confusion would suggest a serious personality disorder at a later developmental age if not done for artistic effect (for example, Picasso). Of course, it is essential to view all child behavior within a developmental perspective. What is usual or normal at one developmental level may be deviant or abnormal at another.

What impresses children will be drawn large, regardless of relative size and position in space. Like the ancient Egyptians who portrayed the husband twice and even three times the size of his mate, children will use size to indicate the dominant family member. Young children have their own ideas regarding perspective. After all, linear perspective was not discovered until Brunelleschi (1377-1446). Children will draw largest the person considered most important, even though others are closer to the viewer. Accordingly, a house in the foreground will be smaller than the person farther away. Eventually, children too will learn about the vanishing point, but until then, as in Chagall's work, dominant figures will loom large, regardless of visual, photographic perspective. The child knows that the person in the distance is just as big as the one at close range.

Fig. 5. Four lines coming from head (five-year-old girl).

Fig. 6. Drawing with belly button (six-year-old boy).

The peculiarities in children's drawings are not wrong. Such a misconception derives from failure to recognize that the world of children differs from our own. When we judge children's behavior by adult standards, it is we who are wrong. Piaget finds in the peculiarities in children's drawings a valuable aid in understanding the child's mental life. The intellectual realism that characterizes the drawings "extends beyond the sphere of drawing"; children's reality is "the outcome of [their] own mental construction . . . (Piaget 1955, p. 189)."

Comparison between Piaget's stages and the evolution of drawing behavior

There is a concordance between the evolution of drawing behavior and the stages of cognitive development as formulated by Piaget.

During the first year, the child does not draw. The crayon is brought to the mouth. Hand-to-mouth reaction predominates.

Scribbling begins at about 13 months of age. Children delight in watching movement leave its marks on a surface. Sense and motion combine to intensify pleasure. Piaget has called the stage that prevails before age two *sensorimotor*.

Piaget considers children from two to seven years of age to be *preoperational* in their thinking. He has divided the stage into a first, preconceptual phase from two to four years of age, and a second, intuitive phase from four to seven years of age. During the first phase, usually between the ages of three and four, the child discovers the ability to produce a pictorial symbol. The child may name the symbol drawn, but the adult may not recognize it. Unrealistic colors are used at this time and well into the intuitive phase of this preoperational stage. The child has now crossed the bridge into Luquet's stage of representational drawing. There will be some backsliding into the earlier scribbling stage, but the direction is toward more representational drawing. During these years, symbolism is at its peak in play, in drawing, and in the acquisition of the auditory symbols that constitute the material of receptive and expressive speech. In drawing, the child is guided by what is known, not by what is actually seen:

> The object simply serves as a cue, not as a visual model to be reproduced. The child draws an internal model. If the drawing is of a person, the result will be identical whether the person is actually present or not. If you sit in front of a child under seven and offer a profile view, you will be drawn standing and full-face. (Di Leo 1977, p. 48)

Piaget regards the intellectual realism described by Luquet as "one of the most important phenomena of the mental life of the child between the years of 3 and 7 (Piaget 1955, p. 189)."

Children are highly subjective during the entire preoperational stage. Human figure drawings tell us more about the artist than about the subject drawn. The head is huge because it is our most important part. It sees, talks, eats, hears, laughs, and cries. Children are absolutely right. What are we without our heads?

Between seven and twelve years of age, egocentricity gradually gives way to an increasingly objective and realistic appraisal of the world. Children are beginning to realize that the moon does not follow them as they walk. They can now see themselves in another's place; they can classify on the basis of less specific aspects than before. This is Piaget's stage of *concrete operations* and Luquet's stage of *visual realism*.

Drawings are now more realistic as an attempt is made to draw what is actually seen. As children mature into this period, body parts will be in better proportion; people will no longer be visible through walls of their houses; profiles will no longer show two eyes and two noses.

In cognitive development, children are acquiring concepts of conservation of volume and weight and are no longer deceived by irrelevant changes in shape. Now they know that the amount of water does not increase because it is poured into a taller container. The ability to listen to another's viewpoint, to place one's self in the other's position, is reflected in being able to tell which is the right and left side of the person facing the child.

In drawings too, children can cross over and draw the right side of their body on the right of the figure and not on the mirror-image side. This ability to cross over is not generally observed before age seven. In Di Leo (1977), there is a drawing by a boy whose right side was poorly developed because of hemiplegia, a paralysis of that side. In his self-portrait, he drew that side smaller, crossing over instead of drawing the mirror-image side of his defective limbs.

To correct visual first impressions, to think it out before responding, and to reverse numbers are among the hallmarks of the stage of visual realism and concrete operations that herald the advance into the maturity of *formal operations*. This stage is attained sometime after age 12. It is marked by the ability to think in abstract terms and to reason logically, arriving at conclusions by inductive as well as deductive reasoning. During this period, children tend to lose interest in their art productions as they begin to view them with an objectively critical eye.

All aspects of behavior—motor, emotional, cognitive, social, developmental—are not only interrelated, but indivisible. Our limitations require that we discuss one aspect at a time while attempting to keep the whole in mind.

Drawings are studied as manifestations of the cognitive and affective life. In drawing the single human figure, children are generally telling what they know. Human figure drawings are widely recognized as expressions of cognitive development, for example, in the Goodenough-Harris test (Goodenough 1926, Harris 1963). However, when we ask a child to draw her or his family, the child's feelings are likely to be mobilized. The drawing may be inferior quantitatively to the single figure, but it tends to reveal the child's concept of family members and her or his own status within the family context. A dominant parent will loom conspicuously larger than a physically larger mate. Jealousy may be expressed by drawing the new baby as a worm (Di Leo 1970, p. 197).

The chronological ages indicated in Table 1 for the various stages are variable and approximate. The sequence of stages, however, is invariant. Pressure and practice may seem to alter the order and anticipate achievements, but conceptual development follows laws of orderly growth. In the normal child, intervention that aims at accelerating the developmental process is likely to rob the child of the thrill of discovery and the feeling of self-affirmation. Besides, it is doubtful whether a concept can be assimilated before the mental structure is ready to operate at that level.

In evaluating children's behavior, developmental age is a more valid criterion than chronological age. The same principle applies to children's artwork.

Encouraging creative self-expression

Lowenfeld and Brittain (1975) have been most effective in showing how art can and should play a vital role in the education of young children. Too often, family and teachers inhibit children's creativity. These authorities stress the

Table 1. Stages of Development

Approximate Ages	Drawing Stages (Luquet)	Drawing Stages (Lowenfeld)	Intellectual Stages (Piaget)	Characteristics of Drawings
Fifteen months to three or four years	Le dessin involon- taire (involuntary design)	Scribbling	Sensorimotor to two years	Zigzags, whorls, and circles
			Preoperational/ Preconceptual from ages two to four	May begin to name scribbles
Three or four to seven years	Intellectual realism	Preschematic	Preoperational/ Intuitive	Subjective. First representations are made. Children draw what they know, not what they see. Color is unrealistic; objects are arranged randomly; symbols are named. Children cannot visualize things from vantage point of others.
Seven to twelve years	Visual realism	Schematic (7-9) Dawning realism (9-12)	Concrete operations	Children develop form concepts, or schemas, which they use repeatedly. Objects are often arranged on a base line. Visual first impressions are corrected. Children want to draw things as they actually are. Later in the stage there is more self-consciousness and children attempt to draw smaller and with more detail.

Although chronological ages may vary, the sequence of stages does not.

relationship between rich sensory experience and mental growth and spontaneous expression, while distinguishing between creative self-expression and boundless, undisciplined ego expansion.

In agreement with most investigators, they decry the use of coloring books because they block the creative impulse. Although coloring books keep children quietly occupied, they do not teach children fine motor control. It is far better to have children draw their own pictures and color them by staying within their own lines. Workbooks with schematic birds or similar figures that are to be colored five in red and four in blue do not teach number concepts; instead, they teach children to draw schematic birds in place of their own concepts. (For more about these and other stifling pseudo-educational devices, see Di Leo 1977).

In encouraging creative self-expression, we must recognize that talent cannot flourish without discipline, devotion, and training. But before children can take on direction without impairment of their imagination and natural inventiveness, they will have to be allowed considerable freedom during their earlier years. Aesthetic awareness can be fostered indirectly by exposure to an environment rich in opportunities to experience sensory phenomena of all kinds. Adults should gently guide awareness by wisely choosing the experiences they provide for children.

The aesthetic sense is not inborn, yet every human being is endowed with the potential to develop it. It is never too early to begin. This does not mean dragging bored, reluctant young children through museums. Experiences are more fruitful when they are pleasurable and involve active participation. Children enjoy doing, especially if encouraged and praised. Nature and human creations offer many life-enhancing sights, sounds, and textures.

Formal art training may be most effective in preadolescence. By that time, if adult standards have not been imposed, children will have acquired a sense of self-affirmation. During adolescence, interest in drawing and painting declines. Graphic activity may become limited to doodling in notebooks. This decline has been attributed to the development of the critical faculty and resultant dissatisfaction with one's work. Talented teenagers will tend to persist in expressing themselves in the visual arts. Others, whose creativity has been fostered during the formative years, will turn to other, more personally appropriate fields for expression of their talents and inclinations—perhaps to science or education or to new areas of human activity.

The common factor in creative expression is the courage to think one's own thoughts and to act upon them, to break with tradition. Clearly, early encouragement to try even the impossible is a positive element in the sustenance of the creative spirit inherent in each of us. Such encouragement must come from nurturing adults: parental figures and teachers.

Although our culture tends to emphasize conformity, children can be encouraged to express originality, to experiment, and to think and act creatively. Creativity enhances self-esteem and strengthens the ego. Such activity especially helps emotionally disturbed individuals. The act of making something original, regardless of its artistic value, effectively externalizes pent-up negative feelings and hostility and, as such, is an aspect of psychiatric treatment.

In drawings, children make personal statements. Studies of family drawings often provide the investigator with revealing clues as to the nature of problems affecting children's well-being. In drawing the family, children are likely to express unwittingly what they are reluctant or unable to verbalize: feelings and impressions regarding the significant people in their lives. Burns and Kaufman (1970) have used the technique of having the child draw all members of the family doing something. This method helps diagnose behavior difficulties stemming from disturbed family relationships.

Creative activity, beyond its value to the individual, plays a role in human affairs. Society owes its progress to the contributions of those who have dared to think and to act differently, often at great sacrifice to themselves (Read 1966).

The arts—music, dance, and visual—are a unifying force in society. The universality of children's earliest pictorial forms, clearly demonstrated by Kellogg (1967) and others, attests to the basic unity of humanity. The emergence of the circle from the kinesthetic scribblings and its symbolic use by children everywhere and by early humans lends impressive support to Jung's theory (1977) of archetypes, or primordial images expressive of the collective unconscious. The circle and a few lines are the universal patterns whereby all normal children symbolize the human figure and the sun. The orderly progression of sequences in the development of graphic activity is but one aspect of the natural growth of body, mind, and emotions. When the normal course of development is hindered, starved, or deviated by negative forces, the normal drive toward self-expression, adaptation, and resumption of progress is suppressed or distorted.

Children's graphic activity should be appreciated and encouraged because of its universal appeal and its potential for creative expression. Few children will become tomorrow's famous sculptors or painters, but all can be influenced to sustain the confidence and daring to be creative, if not in the arts, then in other fields of human endeavor. The issue is not the product, but the feeling of satisfaction derived from an enjoyed and appreciated activity.

How to nurture development through drawing: suggestions and cautions

Provide abundant cheap paper. Newsprint is ideal for large drawings made on the floor. Children are thus able to move both small and large muscles freely as vision and the whole body become involved in the drawing. For tabletop drawing, use ordinary 8½ × 11 inch paper.

Young children generally prefer large crayons until they are able to guide a pencil. Finger painting and brush painting are more difficult to control and do not lend themselves to portraying detail as can be done with line drawings.

Show interest and praise judiciously. Children can tell if the adult is praising or flattering.

Do not tear up or throw away the product, but instead, allow the child to make the decision. Never discard a drawing in the child's presence.

Demonstrate the use of materials but refrain from telling what to do and how to do it.

Do not draw pictures for a child. This will discourage the child's own effort because your drawing is likely to be superior to the child's. Do not comply when the child asks you to draw; instead, encourage the child to do it.

Never have children copy someone else's drawing.

Do not give coloring books. Children cannot benefit from filling in something drawn by someone else. The child should create a personal image. The contention that coloring books promote better control of the writing instrument by training the child to stay within the lines is not valid. The same purpose can be achieved by having children color and stay within the lines of their own drawings.

Do not teach or encourage the making of stick people or other trick schematic figures. These simplified adult tricks tend to discourage children from expressing their own concepts of a person, animal, or object.

Do not try to teach the concept of body image by having children draw a person and then telling them what to add that has been omitted. The concept of body image is acquired from the interaction of intrinsic forces with the environment. Children's drawings of people express the concept as they know and feel it at that time. Teaching body image by drawing is a reversal of the process. As children mature, their drawings will express the developmental changes that are occurring.

Representative drawings made at various stages should be preserved for interesting, informative, and often delightful comparison with those made as each child grows older.

Many children will spontaneously talk about their drawing. If they do not, refrain from asking, "What is it?" One may, however, say, "Tell me something about it," or some similar general remark that does not suggest an answer or put the child on the spot.

Do not deprive children of the thrill of making their own discoveries. This is particularly apropos of the once-in-a-lifetime thrill of having suddenly become aware that a casually drawn circle can become a symbol, heralding the passage from kinesthetic scribbling to representational drawing.

Do not prefer one child's drawing to another's.

There are many more *don'ts* than *do's* in these suggestions because of the tendency of adults to ask too many questions and to believe that they are teaching by correcting or showing. Although done with the best of intentions, nevertheless, such actions impede self-expression and the natural will to be creative. We must avoid identifying with those adults whom Grozinger (1955) had in mind when he stated that, as with a lasso, the adult tries to catch the child and pull him over to our side.

References

Burns, R. C., and Kaufman, S. H. *Kinetic Family Drawings (K-F-D)*. New York: Brunner/Mazel, 1970.

Claparède, E. *Psychologie de l'Enfant et Pedagogie Expérimentale*. Paris: Delachaux & Niestlé, 1946.

Di Leo, J. H. *Young Children and Their Drawings*. New York: Brunner/Mazel, 1970.

Di Leo, J. H. *Children's Drawings as Diagnostic Aids*. New York: Brunner/Mazel, 1973.

Di Leo, J. H. *Child Development: Analysis and Synthesis*. New York: Brunner/Mazel, 1977.

Eng, H. *The Psychology of Children's Drawings*. 2nd ed. London: Routledge & Kegan Paul, 1954.

Freud, S. *A General Introduction to Psychoanalysis*. Garden City, N.Y.: Doubleday, 1943.

Goodenough, F. L. *Measurement of Intelligence by Drawings*. New York: World Book Co., 1926.

Grozinger, W. *Scribbling, Drawing, Painting*. New York: Praeger, 1955.

Harris, D. B. *Children's Drawings as Measures of Intellectual Maturity*. New York: Harcourt, Brace & World, 1963.

Jung, C. G. *The Symbolic Life*. Bollingen Series XX. Princeton, N.J.: Princeton University Press, 1977.

Kellogg, R. *The Psychology of Children's Art*. New York: Random House, 1967.

Lansing, K. M. *Art, Artists, and Art Education*. New York: McGraw-Hill, 1969.

Levinstein, S. *Kinderzeichnungen bis zum 14 Lebensjahr*. Leipzig: R. Voigtlander Verlag, 1905.

Lowenfeld, V., and Brittain, W. L. *Creative and Mental Growth*. 6th ed. New York: Macmillan, 1975.

Luquet, G. H. *Les Dessins d'un Enfant: Étude Psychologique*. Paris: Librarie Félix Alcan, 1913.

Piaget, J. *The Language and Thought of the Child*. Cleveland: World, 1955.

Piaget, J., and Inhelder, B. *Mental Imagery in the Child*. New York: Basic Books, 1971.

Read, H., ed. *Art and Society*. New York: Schocken Books, 1966.

Read, H. "Art as a Unifying Principle in Education." In *Child Art: The Beginnings of Self-Affirmation*, ed. H. Lewis. 2nd ed. Berkeley, Calif.: Diablo Press, 1973.

Ricci, C. *L'Arte dei Bambini*. Bologna: Zanichelli Editore, 1887.

Rouma, G. *El Lenguaje Gráfico del Niño*. Havana: Gutierrez y Comp., 1919.

3
Fostering Creativity

Two-year-old Mia watches intently as the dough clay oozes out from between the fingers of her clenched fist. Then she breaks off a bit of the soft mass and plops it into her mouth.

At the kindergarten chalkboard, David grabs a thick rod of orange chalk. He vigorously scribbles several circular patterns over one another. Then he claps at his work with a handy eraser and grins as the chalk dust begins to fly.

In the art room, seven-year-old On Fan splatters droplets of each of the available tempera paint colors onto her paper. Then she carefully trails a brush through the paint and stands back to admire the rainbow-hued pattern she has created. Discovering an animal-like form, she purposefully outlines it with black crayon.

Here we see how the sensuous quality of art media can arouse young children's curiosities. Children are enticed by the endless play opportunities of colorful and malleable materials. Thus, Mia, David, and On Fan engage in the first exploratory stage of the creative process.

What is the creative process? How do young children engage in it? These questions will be discussed in this chapter. In addition, we shall focus on the teacher's role in establishing a climate which supports and encourages child participation in creative art.

The creative process

The process of creating implies producing something that was not there before. The creative process for child artists is "a mental process that directs the child's eye and hand" and differs according to the approach of each child to a particular problem (see Chapter 2 by Joseph Di Leo, p. 5). Other authorities have detailed various steps in the creative process. There is a fairly consistent pattern in which each step has certain identifiable characteristics.

The creative process usually begins with a time of playing around and exploring. This first step is a time for trying out and for manipulation of ideas or materials before the creator focuses on how to solve a particular problem (Foshay 1961; Mendelowitz 1963; Montgomery 1973).

The next step is focusing. Of the many possibilities sensed in the exploring phase, one is finally selected and pursued. To focus means to commit oneself to a particular choice or a prism through which to tell one's story (Mukerji 1976; Foshay 1961). Focusing is a highly conscious act which leads to the next step, producing.

Producing is the easily recognized working stage during which the creator, using whatever technical skills are required and available, carries out the project. It is a time of intense problem solving, imagination, and interim analysis.

The creator stops when satisfied with the solution to a problem or expression of an idea. This fourth step, *stopping,* can also be combined with *evaluating* or *reworking.*

In describing the creative process as it relates to visual art, Lowenfeld and Brittain (1975) state that it is frequently difficult to pinpoint when one step ends and another begins. They claim, as do others, that vacillation between the steps may occur. Exploring, focusing, producing, and reworking steps may be repeated before children arrive at the stopping phase.

The steps in the creative process, and the variations which may occur within them, cut across all the arts and apply to artists of all ages. However, younger children spend most of their time with art materials in exploratory play—the first step.

Children engaged in art activities spontaneously move back and forth between exploring and producing. Yet, in the following descriptions of children in action, it is often possible to identify the stages in the creative process.

Exploring

Children manipulate materials and experiment with them during the exploring step in the creative process. They discover the possibilities and limitations of various materials. The explorations become additionally valuable when children share these discoveries with peers.

Mixing their own tempera paint from the colored powders was a popular exploratory activity for the five-year-old children in Ms. R's room, but silver paint was their favorite. One day Michael and Tony decided to find out what would happen if they mixed silver powder with the other colors. Of course, when the boys tried it, all the paints turned glittery. When Ms. R pointed out the boys' discovery, the rest of the group quickly became interested in silvery paint. Silver-tinged red blobs, silvery black squiggles, and glittery multicolored striped paintings appeared daily. The whole class explored, experimented, and discovered.

In the process of exploring art materials, children discover a variety of techniques for using particular items and often develop skills needed to move on to other steps in the creative process. For example, when different types of papers are available, children will try tearing, then cutting, rolling, bending, twisting, or crumpling. Children will discover that some papers respond more easily to one of these processes than others.

A group of young children was busy pasting bits of colored paper onto a sheet of brown wrapping paper. They selected from a variety of torn and cut shapes arranged in the compartments of a cast-off candy box. As Rosa pasted bits of colored tissue, some became quite moist and scrunched up into clumps rather than remaining flat. "It looks like a flower," she said to Paulo, her

Children manipulate materials and experiment with them during the exploring step in the creative process.

neighbor. "Let's make more." Rosa and Paulo then continued to paste many colored tissue papers, each time purposefully scrunching them up to look like flowers. Exploration and discovery—a peak experience leading to production.

These two examples and the three at the beginning of this chapter show how much discovery can take place during the exploratory phase. This step in the process occurs with each new material.

For most young children under four years of age, the creative process begins and ends with exploring. The windowsill of the three-year-old children's room was covered with a melange of artwork: dry bits of clay in odd shapes, a few glued-together wood assemblages, assorted collages, and crayoned scribbles. "It is not important to these children to really finish artwork," explained the teacher. "They enjoy the process of playing with the materials, but usually forget to take home the things they have worked on."

Focusing

In the example of Rosa and the paper flowers, we saw how easily young children slip from the exploring to the producing stage without passing through the focusing step of more mature creators. Here we see how young children

Teachers of young children can tell when they are ready to plan for creating or constructing items which require both logical thought and technical skill.

differ from older children and adults. Very young children do not exhibit the conscious purposefulness of the focusing stage. They are more intuitive at this stage and frequently change direction midway through their art projects.

Producing

With more experience, children gradually become more interested in creating a final product with the art materials. As they reach the developmental stage of symbolic representation and are better able to control particular art materials, children's intuitive efforts at creating art projects become more purposeful.

Four-year-old Tricia paints her paper over and over again, one color covering another. Finally she covers everything with black and explains to her teacher, "This is me when I was hiding under my bed."

As five-year-old Timmy paints a large red circle and adds radiating lines, he tells his easel partner about the sun he is making. A few minutes later the sun becomes a clock as he paints in a few numerals and two clock hands.

Both Tricia and Timmy have moved to the producing step of the creative process because their work has become purposeful; their act of creating seems to stimulate further creation. Also, there does not seem to be any real focus or systematic plan of production, unlike that which we find in the work of older artists. The producing step for four- and five-year-old children frequently seems primarily intuitive.

Teachers of young children can tell when they are ready to plan for creating or constructing items which require both logical thought and technical skill. From observing pupils, we know that some children will be able to focus on a plan and create items such as a mural, masks, doll beds, or puppets. Carla's first-grade teacher knew that Carla was able to carry out her own plans for making many items. When a box of Styrofoam scraps was brought to school, Carla explored the small pieces for a short time. Then, as she picked up a handful, she announced, "I am going to put these together with toothpicks to make a puppet." Carla was so successful in creating her puppet that several classmates joined her to make Styrofoam characters for a play they wrote. Joseph extended the process further by adding pipe cleaners to his character's head for antlers, and he used a small red bead for a nose to make the puppet look like Rudolph.

Like Carla and Joseph, many five- to eight-year-old children are sufficiently adept at using art materials to make objects representing their own ideas. This was true of Julio, who had spent much time at the chalkboard. One day the teacher noticed that Julio was drawing a person who had a rather long line protruding from one of his toes. "I wonder who that could be?" she mused. "Oh," responded Julio, "that's my cousin Felipe. He got a splinter in his foot because he walked with no shoes."

When children have reached the step in the creative process at which they are able to produce, they will frequently express the same idea with several materials. For example, seven-year-old Beth was fascinated by the actions of her new kitten, Pitsy Mitsy. Her paintings and drawings were full of Pitsy Mitsy's sleeping and eating. She also made many clay cats. When some of the children in Beth's class decided to make puppets with paper plates, Beth quickly joined them. She chose absorbent cotton balls to glue all over her plate so that the puppet would be as fuzzy as her cat. It was apparent to her teacher that the several ways in which Beth represented the animal helped this child to clarify further her knowledge about the pet and her relationship to it.

When children are in the producing step of the creative process, we see not only their activity and the emerging product, but also at times the fascinating efforts to solve the problems blocking their intentions to express their ideas with art materials.

Stopping

Children stop when they are satisfied with what they have produced. Stopping is not an easy step in the creative process. Other writers on the subject (Mukerji 1976; Foshay 1961) have noted that the act of declaring a project finished leaves one exposed to the outside world. If criticism is leveled during the working stage, one can always claim, "But I'm not finished yet!" The act of stopping proclaims, in essence, "This is the best I can do." The more confident children are in expressive art activities, the easier it is for them to acknowledge their decision to stop.

On the day of the first winter snowfall, four-year-old Tarim purposefully formed moist clay into several balls, then stopped. "I made six snowballs," he announced to no one in particular. "I'm going to let them get hard." Evidently he had explored clay enough times to be able to produce these simple symbols with it and then stop. Tarim had engaged in the complete creative process.

Dahlia and Jenetha decided to make cards for Valentine's Day. These seven-year-old girls had mastered the process of making cardboard printing plates when designing holiday gift-wrap paper in December. The girls discussed their project together and with their teacher. Then they drew designs on cardboard, cut them out, and glued them to small box lids. When the glue was dry, the girls carefully inked their plates and printed the necessary number of cards. They produced to their own satisfaction; their idea was completed; and then they stopped.

Teachers of young children realize that the decision to stop must be the child's. To ask a child who has stopped working to add to what has been created or to evaluate the item for reworking would violate the child's integrity. The teacher will know that some children will stop because they are not satisfied with their work, because they are tired, or simply because they do not go through the entire process, as three-year-old children may do. Therefore, it is important that we do not confuse stopping which takes place as part of the creative process with stopping that occurs for other reasons. The creative process ends when the child wishes to stop.

Even in young children, the progression of the creative process from exploring through producing to finally stopping has a dynamic quality of its own. The exploring phase may appear casual, accidental, or energetic. It may be difficult to tell when the child slips into the producing phase, which may or may not seem purposeful to us. Somehow, the art object takes shape as the child shows new intensity in her or his work. The final phase of stopping usually comes abruptly. The child may say, "I'm done," with a tone of finality tinged with satisfaction. The dynamics of the various phases are inherent in the creative process. What kind of atmosphere or climate can help to foster creativity in young children?

The decision to stop working must be the child's. To ask a child who has stopped to add to what has been created or to evaluate the item for reworking would violate the child's integrity.

A climate for children's expressiveness

The healthy development of children through creative art cannot be fostered in a hostile or emotionally barren environment. It requires a climate of psychological safety to progress down the bumpy roads of children's highly distinctive personal developmental landscapes. There is more to creating a supportive climate for children than approaching them with a general aura of good will.

A climate for creativity and expressiveness is a complex concept. It may help us develop such a climate if we look at its various program components, especially as they relate to young children's art.

Accepting children

We may have a tendency to equate acceptance, especially unconditional acceptance, with an attitude of anything goes—that is, anything short of mayhem. In a classroom reflecting this view, one sees the teacher withdraw from the children during art activities (and also, incidentally, from play) while attending to routine paper duties. This type of teacher accepts the children by leaving them to their own resources and limitations.

At the other end of the spectrum we find a tendency to equate acceptance of children with what we regard as acceptable behavior. In a classroom reflecting this view, one may hear a teacher say, in response to a child's explanation of her picture, "But you really don't want to burn up your family—you love them—don't you?" This type of comment may arise when a teacher finds it difficult to accept the powerful, sometimes desperate, feelings children express in artwork.

Expressing strong feelings through art rather than through destructive acts may provide some catharsis which reduces anxiety and guilt about children's emotions. Teachers who accept the reality of children's feelings can understand children better and help them cope with distressing feelings. Conversely, teachers who accept children's expression of their desires, anticipations, and delights can share, and thus intensify, children's joy.

Teachers have countless opportunities to model an accepting attitude for children. When Patricia derisively called three-year-old Sasha's crayon picture "scribble scrabble," the teacher matter-of-factly commented, "Sasha is hard at work trying out many different crayons. That's exactly how everybody begins—with big, colorful lines." Sasha smiled contentedly; Patricia said "oh," and went off thinking her own thoughts, but perhaps somewhat responsive to the teacher's casual yet positive acceptance of the legitimacy of scribbling in that classroom.

From such small incidents which collectively reveal an attitude, Patricia may realize she is accepted as a person who warrants an explanation, while Sasha may feel the teacher accepts him as he is. When children feel accepted by people who are important to them, they are better able to develop a sense of trust in those people.

Developing a sense of trust

A sense of trust develops from a sense of security. "The general state of trust implies . . . that one has learned to rely on the sameness and continuity of the outer providers . . . (Erikson 1963, p. 248)." An atmosphere of sameness and continuity provides young children with a climate in which they may feel secure. Children then feel that they can depend on a teacher's promise and fairness.

When painting the Tri-Wall boards for the kindergarten doctor's office became the most-demanded activity, the teacher restricted the number of children who could work in the limited space at one time. Randy confirmed the sense of trust which prevailed in the room, "See, Mrs. Markova put our names down to be first painters tomorrow so she doesn't forget. We're first tomorrow."

Children develop a sense of trust in teachers, and teachers also develop trust in their children. Knowing the capabilities and limitations of individual children, a teacher can confidently demonstrate trust in children. Mindy and Samuel can work independently out in the hall decorating the puppet stage. Renata can choose whatever materials she prefers for costumes because she will be careful not to mess up the crowded closet. Jackie, who is still lacking the inner control to work with other children, can be trusted to choose her own dish full of collage materials and to work at her own separate small table.

When children trust, and thus feel secure with their teachers, and when teachers show appropriate trust in children, then children can begin to build confidence in themselves as worthy, competent people.

Building self-confidence

Self-confidence is built on a circular relationship between child and teacher. When the teacher demonstrates confidence in a child, it helps that child develop greater self-confidence.

When four-year-old Rahman was sweeping broad, free strokes of blue, red, and white paint across his paper, the colors inadvertently mixed at various places. Suddenly he stopped, his brush in midair, as he squinted hard at his painting. "Look, it's pink up here and look at this," pointing to a hazy lavender swath. "Yes," said the teacher, catching the excitement of the moment, "and you made them—you made those special colors."

The teacher had a hunch that there was more learning potential in that event than the pleasure of discovery. "Which two colors did you mix to make the pink?" she asked. Without hesitation Rahman responded, "Oh, that's red and white, mixed." "So now you can make pink whenever you want," summarized the teacher. "Yeah," whispered Rahman with a touch of pride and awe, "I'll mix red and white."

In this way the teacher made explicit her confidence that he could repeat purposefully a technique for changing color which he discovered accidentally. Rahman's response highlighted a moment of self-confidence in his ability to control this responsive art medium.

Teachers are often faced with the dilemma of a child's plaintive request: "I can't do it. I don't know how. You make it for me!" followed by a long, drawn-out "Please?" Marissa, who was in the second grade, appealed to her teacher to make her clay dog for her because she felt she did not know how. Her teacher, knowing Marissa was advanced enough to represent her idea of a dog, seized on this opportunity to try to bolster her self-confidence. Sensing that the image of a dog held special meaning for Marissa, the teacher asked, "Do you have a dog?" "Yes, and he's mine. I feed him and everything!" Then ensued an animated discussion about the kind of dog, the shape of his ears, and the bushiness of his tail, as well as some of his habits.

"Well, since he's your dog," said the teacher, "you're the one who knows best what he looks like to you. Let's get an idea about the shape of his head. Is it sort of round or sort of long? Try it with a piece of clay." Once the head, body, and ears were assembled with similar encouragement, the teacher left with a parting reminder about the dog's tail. In the end, Marissa created her dog in clay with growing self-confidence that it was *her* vision of *her* dog. The teacher's confidence in Marissa's ability to visualize her dog and to externalize him in clay was based on the reality that Marissa knew her dog better than anyone else. Marissa's self-confidence and growing autonomy were enhanced in this climate of psychological safety which helped her accomplish her own purpose with the assistance of skillful and purposeful teacher support.

Although this procedure was appropriate for seven-year-old Marissa, it would not be suitable for children who are still at the stage of only manipulating clay. Such children may be given suggestions encouraging them to make balls, long skinny shapes, or flat shapes which they may name if and as they choose. Then they too will gain self-confidence at their level of ability and development.

Appreciating individuality

Undergirding a teacher's acceptance of children, the development of trusting relationships, and the building of self-confidence and autonomy lies our basic appreciation of each child's individuality. In the art program, it also means the appreciation of children's expressiveness when they use art media in personally meaningful ways.

Pascal found that his third-grade teacher appreciated his special interest. Pascal's mother was a dancer-anthropologist, and his father was a drummer. Pascal was caught up in the intensity of the family's preparation for a concert based on material from their study of voodun in the Caribbean.

Understanding Pascal's desire to share in this compelling family involvement, his teacher helped him research ceremonial masks and mask-making. He worked intensively on his individual project while different art activities engaged classmates. This teacher not only appreciated her student's individuality, but also meaningfully helped to cement Pascal's school life and family life through art.

Sometimes children's expressions through art are strongly affected by their surroundings and the expectations of responsible adults in a particular environment. For example, Arun seemed to be two different children, judging by his artwork done in kindergarten and at home. His teacher was understandably concerned during a class project drawing Halloween pumpkins, when Arun reluctantly and carelessly drew a ragged circle, three triangles, and a slash for features, with a few random streaks of orange to satisfy the expectation for coloring the pumpkin. She wondered why he resisted drawing and painting.

When Arun showed his pumpkin to a visitor in his home, she acknowledged it with a noncommital, "So that's what you made in kindergarten?" Later, he brought over a picture drawn at home. It was a vibrant field of subtle color done in colored pencil. The visitor said, "Oh," expressing genuine pleasure and interest. Arun volunteered, "You see, when it starts to get a little bit dark outside, it gets reddish-purple over here; then it gets bluish-purple over there." "Yes, I can see that," commented the visitor. He then offered an explanation which showed his real awareness, sensitivity, and skill. "You see, if you want this kind of purple, you put the red on top of the blue and you get red-purple. If you put blue on top, you get blue-purple and it's more like nighttime. My purple pencil won't make it right." What a far cry from his meaningless pumpkin picture. One can only speculate about why he felt it necessary to restrict to his home his remarkable expressiveness in art.

Teachers appreciate how differently children respond to new art activities just as to any other new experiences. Some children eagerly plunge into new activities, attracted, perhaps, to new materials or the newness of the venture, while other children temporarily hold back. Still others retreat to the safety of the familiar and are reluctant to risk themselves with new materials or processes.

Sensitive teachers trying to provide a climate in which children can take risks in their own ways will accommodate to the differences they observe in children. Three-year-old Magda refused her teacher's invitation to try finger painting. She apparently had the same conflicting feelings she had shown when clay was introduced. She wanted to play with messy materials but was anxious about getting carried away in her play and becoming too dirty. Her response to the invitation was to run away and play with the little cars across the room.

Eventually, she drove her car toward the finger painting area while accompanying herself with a steady, persistent engine sound of zh—zh—zh. She barely glanced at the children who were finger painting, then turned and raced back to the block area. Once again Magda approached and stopped her engine sounds. She looked at the painters with furtive glances, pretending to examine the wheels on her car at the same time. The teacher, noting Magda's interest and reluctance, decided to give her more time. Her only comment that day was, "When you decide you want to finger paint, you can pick the color you want."

After a few days, Magda announced, "I want green." The teacher had read her nonverbal behavior correctly; her individual pattern of response had been respected.

These sketches of teacher-child interactions suggest specific ways teachers can demonstrate acceptance of children, develop trusting relationships, build self-confidence and autonomy, and appreciate individuality in young children. In our awareness of these components of the environment, as well as in our understanding of their constant interplay, we can build a climate of psychological safety—a climate for expressiveness in art.

As our understanding of child development grows, as our knowledge of the creative process in art expands, and as our ability to create a nurturing climate deepens, we will see children flourish as they grow. We learn from them as they grow.

Adult as explorer

As teachers, we not only learn *from* children, we also learn *with* them. Therefore, we seek to refresh and renew ourselves professionally and to become more aware and sensitive in teaching young children. Art lends itself especially well to adult exploration and renewal.

Teachers explore art

We can learn about processes and materials that are new to us or with which we have had little or no recent experience. After our own first-hand encounters with them, we will be more confident when our children explore and use them. Also, we can better prepare the materials and more effectively guide children. We may see greater potential in certain materials when we try them out under experienced workshop leaders. We are then in a better position to help children stretch themselves through art as well as to protect our facilities and equipment from disaster such as that which occurs in pouring plaster down the drain. Teachers need the security of feeling increasingly confident in their professional roles.

Art also has a high potency for enabling us to renew and deepen the impact of the creative act on our own levels and on our own lives. When we engage in art activity in adult classes or teacher workshops, we are alert to the emotional quality of our involvement. New materials attract us, but we hesitate to try the unknown. We know the uncertainty and sense of discomfort when we cannot settle on an idea to pursue. Suddenly there is the excitement of the moment of decision; we cannot wait to plunge into work, and we labor intensely as the work takes shape. We become frustrated because we lack the technique to do what we want, and angry when we are interrupted. There is also the moment of anxiety. Will others appreciate our work? There is a sense of release when the work is done—a feeling of accomplishment when effort and persistence show in improved control. Finally, we are proud of our own growth in expressiveness through art. When we renew and strengthen our sensitivity to the art experience through our own explorations, we can better serve children in their learning experiences through art.

Parents explore art

Schools may also offer parents the opportunity to understand the role of art in their children's education by arranging parent workshops, preferably in their children's classrooms. Some of the best open discussions about children and learning occur when people work together with materials in a congenial climate. Parents can rediscover a sense of pleasure and accomplishment while gaining an understanding of what children learn through the art curriculum in a school or child care center.

When parents' work is displayed in their children's rooms with inscriptions such as, "by Janika's mother," or "by Gilberto's grandfather," the children are proud and delighted. Adults who become explorers in the creative process with art materials are better able to appreciate children's explorations and facilitate their progress in learning through art.

Guiding and facilitating children's art expression

A broad foundation supports an art program; we see only a small part of it during children's art activity. The teacher's foundation embraces her or his knowledge of children; a commitment to certain values; careful, intelligent planning; and preparation of the environment for learning through creative art. We see teachers facilitate children's participation and guide and instruct children as they engage in art.

Organize space

Although all classrooms have space problems, the space can be made more attractive, orderly, and inviting for artwork if furniture and equipment are arranged into functional centers or areas of interest.

One type of arrangement separates wet from dry materials. For example, clay and paint centers can be placed near the room's water source. If there is no sink or lavatory in the room, then makeshift arrangements with buckets of water which are filled daily will help.

Because woodworking and block building tend to be noisy, it is desirable to arrange these centers away from quieter activities where children draw or cut and paste. Sometimes children as young as four years of age, as well as older ones, may help determine where particular centers should be located and the reasons for such decisions. For example, a kindergarten teacher, introducing the woodworking bench, held a discussion with the children about where it should be placed. They wisely considered safety and noise factors in making their decision. Some first-grade children planning a mural decided the floor space in the room was inadequate, so one child suggested moving the paper out into the corridor.

Sometimes teachers separate art areas from each other by using low, portable room dividers, available from commercial suppliers or easily made by teachers, parents, or custodians. Other teachers place bookcases, the piano, or tables in positions that create boundaries for centers of interest.

In planning the placement of centers for art activity, it is advisable to consider the source of natural light in the room. Children are likely to be more comfortable if they do not face directly into strong sunlight when they work.

After each center has been established, it helps to have all the necessary materials nearby. Brushes, paints, mixing pans, and paper can be kept at the paint center. Airtight containers of clay, boards, sponges, sticks, wire, and rolling pins can be placed at the clay center.

Lack of storage space is a frequent problem in early childhood classrooms. In organizing space for art, the teacher considers practical places to store materials. Imaginative teachers have found several ways to create storage space.

- Label cardboard or plastic shoe boxes and arrange them on bookshelves, windowsills, or counter tops that children can reach. Simple pictures can be labels for young children.
- Make adjustable shelves with cinder blocks to support lumber or heavy corrugated board (Tri-Wall).
- Place plastic dishpans or attractively covered cartons on top of children's coatracks for storing teacher's supplies.
- Cover a wall area with pegboard and suspend heavy shopping bags or see-through plastic bags from hooks inserted in the board. Hang smocks in the same fashion.
- Screw metal coat hooks into wooden moldings for suspending storage bags or smocks.
- Use the back of the piano or bookcase for hanging a shoe bag. Its pockets can hold many small items.
- Pierce an inverted small cardboard box or egg carton for use as a handy scissor or brush rack.
- Attach a roll of burlap, felt, or strip of cork to a vertical surface which children can reach. Keep a supply of needles threaded with yarn inserted in this oversize pincushion.
- Use divided frozen food trays or a revolving lazy Susan to hold miscellaneous small items.
- Make excellent containers for crayons or chalk out of discarded berry baskets or margarine cups. A label or clip clothespin painted the color of the contents helps children locate colors.
- Use small detergent or cosmetic squeeze bottles as dispensers for paint or glue purchased in quantity.

Provide materials

What criteria can assist us in choosing suitable art materials for young children? What kinds and variety will suit their developmental needs?

Safety

Be sure that commercial art materials or appropriate substitutes are safe for children. Labels may indicate that materials are toxic. Will the item be likely to cause splinters, pierce the skin, or cause abrasions? Will the attractive glitter stick under fingernails? Are the fumes from a spray irritating? Will a two-year-old child's tongue-test transfer color from the object to the mouth? Adults who know children's capabilities will judiciously offer items such as toothpicks, empty cans, tacks, pins, and staplers.

Teachers who first try new materials for learning art processes will become aware of applicable safety factors. Most young children can learn to be careful workers when they understand hazards. A teacher demonstrating how to use a crosscut saw might ask "What can happen if your finger is too near the blade?" or when discussing how to use scissors "How can you hide the point in your fist so that it cannot hurt anyone while you are walking with it?" Two- and three-year-old children will usually need to have adults set rules, for example, "We don't put needles in our mouths because we can hurt ourselves," or "Clay is for modeling, not for eating." Children four years of age and older can cooperatively decide on rules and regulations for safe handling of tools, materials, and equipment. However, older children may still need verbal reminders or simple signs.

Although food items may be safe, they are not appropriate for art experiences. Because many other materials are available, it is unwise to waste food by using it for art. Teachers will find that many of the free, inexpensive, or recycled materials listed at the end of this section offer excellent alternatives.

Developmental appropriateness

Art materials that enable children to express ideas easily meet developmental needs best. Drawing tools such as crayons, markers, and chalk should be thick enough for young hands to grasp without breaking too readily. The tools should mark clearly and flow easily. Paints are basic art materials because they offer children the most fluidity. The best media and materials are those that are the least structured and can be used by children in many ways. Raw materials such as natural clay or beach sand offer nonstructured possibilities to children. Many commercial art materials are also appropriate if children are given opportunities to explore different ways of using them. Those items which must have rules attached to their use limit children's chances to learn through discovery as they work with them. Materials that children can form or assemble in their own ways are best, including modeling clay, paper, wood scraps, recycled found materials, and a variety of items from the natural environment. Chapter 4 discusses specifics about the kind and quality of each medium.

Materials which children can form or assemble in their own ways are best, including modeling clay, paper, wood scraps, recycled found materials, and a variety of items from the natural environment.

In providing materials which are developmentally appropriate for their group, teachers also look at individual needs. Can Duncan cope with the openness of sand, or must he first be given rules for working with it? Does Mark, who has cerebral palsy, need a piece of foam rubber wrapped around the chalk to aid his grasp? Will Resa, like many three-year-old children, be confused when offered too many choices, or can she cope with variety? Too much variety may be developmentally inappropriate for some children, yet for other children it can breathe new life into an art program.

Why and when to provide a variety of materials for early childhood art deserves thoughtful consideration. After children have had opportunities to explore the basic expressive materials, varieties of the basics can be introduced, providing the children do not become confused. Two- and three-year-old children and some insecure older children may still need consistency because sameness and simplicity provide a sense of security. Observant teachers will notice when a child begins to lose interest in using art materials or when a child keeps repeating the same crayon or paint symbols daily. Then it may be time to offer that child the stimulation contained in a change of medium or novel material. Teachers will offer more variety to children whose intellectual development and technical skills demonstrate a need for the greater challenge which comes from using more complex materials. For example, children who have mastered simple sewing techniques on punched cardboard or Styrofoam trays may be ready for the challenge provided by stitching nylon mesh or burlap.

If a variety of materials is available, especially to children five years of age and older, they can discover alternative ways of accomplishing similar tasks. For example, if glue does not hold, children may try tape or a stapler. If other fibers are available in addition to yarn, children will experiment and discover possibilities for knotting, stitching, or weaving with each. Children, finding some materials more satisfying than others, are more apt to use them to express ideas. Thus, the addition of sewing supplies may give seven-year-old Leslie an opportunity to stitch, rather than draw or paint. Paul might find that constructing with wood scraps is more satisfying than using paper or cardboard. With variety, older children come to understand that color, line, form, and texture can be expressed through different materials. Teachers may find that when they have a variety of materials available for art, the base from which they can connect to other curriculum areas becomes broader. The ideas for curriculum-related art projects discussed in Chapter 5 indicate the necessity for an array of materials with which children can choose to create.

Cost and availability

A variety of developmentally appropriate materials for children's art does not necessarily cost more. Chapter 4 offers suggestions for homemade substitutes for expensive products. Many of the items on the following list can substitute for expensive purchases. Such materials may be right at your fingertips while others can be contributed by parents and friends. Children can collect a variety of things from their environment to incorporate into their artwork. When items come from their own collection, children tend to demonstrate increased respect for materials. The following list may be useful as a starting point for a collection of found materials for art activities:

paper cups	bottle caps
paper plates	soda carton carriers
paper towels	pie pans
paper napkins	meat and fruit trays
tissues	gift boxes
newspaper	clothespins
paper bags	toothpicks
magazines	rubber bands
greeting cards	coffee stirrers
coupons	ice cream sticks
catalogs	nails and screws
shopping bags	pebbles and stones
comic books	shells
jar tops	feathers
salt boxes	balloons
empty cans (edges smoothed)	bobby or hair pins
spray can tops	sandwich bags
plastic lids	broken jewelry
plastic containers	buttons
plastic wrap	lollipop sticks
tongue depressors	thread and yarn
gift ribbon	soap flakes
sponges	wire
food color	old toothbrushes
seeds	spools
milk cartons	frozen food trays
paper tubes	candles
cardboard	meat trays
waxed paper	fruit trays
foils	coffee cans
cotton	sawdust
paperclips	sequins
squeeze bottles	beads
egg cartons	Styrofoam
cereal boxes	

Appendix A lists sources from which many items can be obtained inexpensively.

It will not be difficult to select or add other appropriate materials of your choice. With a little time, a few ideas, and a bit of imagination, children will use these materials alone or in combination to experience the art processes described in Chapter 4.

Housekeeping supplies

To work creatively with art materials, children need to be freed from constraints and worry related to keeping themselves and their work spaces clean. Children will need smocks to protect clothing, supplies for covering work surfaces, and tools for cleaning. Children will also need to know where to place work in progress for safekeeping and where wet items can be left to dry. Providing these items is part of the teacher's responsibility as guide and facilitator.

Smocks offering good protection can be made from discarded shirts or blouses. Smocks worn backwards provide the best coverage for clothing. Teachers can cut long sleeves off to within a few inches of the shoulder seams. A large button can be sewn at the neck edge of a shirt smock and a buttonhole or loop made to fit it on the opposite side. Children as young as three years of age can help each other into these smocks. Sometimes teachers or parents sew the top edge of an old towel or washcloth on a shirt smock front. This provides extra absorbency and is convenient for wiping hands.

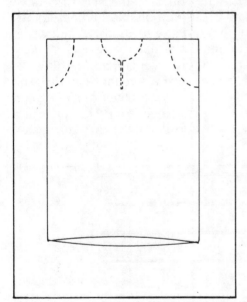

Fig. 7. Plastic trash bag smock.   *Fig. 8. Newspaper smock.*

In emergencies, extra art smocks can be made easily from either large plastic trash bags or newspaper.

(1) Cut openings for the child's head and arms at the closed end of a plastic trash bag (see Figure 7).

(2) Staple together a triple thickness of opened newspaper. Roll a small sheet of newspaper into a neckband and staple it to the smock with enough room to fit over a child's head (see Figure 8).

Table and floor protectors can be made of newspapers. However, plastic dropcloths, shower curtains, or inexpensive plastic tablecloths placed on work surfaces before children begin their art activity will provide the best protection from wet and sticky artwork.

Cleanup supplies should always include a bucket of sponges. They are easy for children to use and can be rinsed and used again. When liquid detergent or scouring powder is available, children can rub it into stubborn stains made by paint, glue, or crayon. A simple way for children to remove crayon marks from laminated surfaces is to rub them with scraps of dry felt. Sometimes bits of facial tissue work as well. Liquid detergent or soap flakes can be added to tempera paints to make their removal easier, especially from clothing.

Drying racks are convenient to have in early childhood classrooms. However, the commercial type can be expensive. An inexpensive substitute can be assembled in the same manner as a Tri-Wall bookshelf. Cardboard is placed on top of four brick or block supports (one in each corner). Several layers are built so paintings can be left on the shelves for drying (Figure 9). Two other methods for drying paintings are (1) hanging paintings on a clothesline suspended above the head of the tallest adult, and (2) using portable folding clothes driers. However, paintings can drip in both of these methods. Windowsills can also be used, especially for drying three-dimensional artwork.

Masonite boards cut in ten-inch squares are convenient for transporting wet or unfinished clay work and assemblages to a place where they can dry. The children can work directly on the boards when they start their modeling and construction. These boards can frequently be obtained from scrap piles at a lumberyard or purchased inexpensively. Foam core board or heavy corrugated cardboard can also be used.

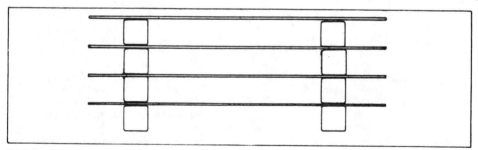

Fig. 9. Drying rack.

Miscellaneous supplies

Other useful art supplies are paper towels, plastic trash bags, and large empty cartons. The cartons can serve as wastebaskets or be inverted and cut at an angle to make table easels. Placed on top of one another, the cartons become display kiosks for the children's artwork. Cafeteria trays have many uses. Rubber gloves to protect allergic skin and goggles to wear at the woodworking bench may also be necessary.

Provide time for in-depth experiences

To become expressive with art materials young children need time to develop manual dexterity and skills and to explore materials in depth. Initially, children will manipulate new materials, taking time to explore the unfamiliar. The amount of time children need to explore particular materials depends on the materials, whether the children have had previous satisfying experiences with them, and frequently whether use of the items offers opportunities for socialization. Thus, children who receive pleasure from the sensory stimulation afforded by clay or finger paint may need to spend more time with those media than with crayon. Children who have had artwork displayed in the classroom will be likely to want time to use the same medium for other expression. Some children, knowing that friends are working in a particular center or with particular materials, will want to join them.

Children need to repeat art processes over a period of time in order to become competent with, and feel secure about, using the materials to express ideas and feelings. Four- and five-year-old children who have many opportunities to paint will frequently move rapidly from manipulative scribbling to expressive symbolic or schematic representations. If children are given time for in-depth manipulation of clay, the same kind of development can often be observed. Repeated opportunities to engage in processes such as cutting, pasting, stitching, and printmaking are essential.

Once children have practiced new skills, they will try other techniques. For example, after several opportunities to squeeze and pound clay, a child might begin to roll snake-like forms, make depressions with fingers, or break off pieces and put them together in new ways.

Danny's painting indicates how time can provide opportunity for children's growth and expression in art. When he entered kindergarten, he had already attended nursery school for two years. He had many opportunities for painting with water and tempera paint both at home and at nursery school. Unlike many of his classmates, he approached the easel during the first weeks in kindergarten with confidence and purpose. Although Danny did not yet create many symbols which represented ideas, he formed colorful geometric designs, manipulating his brush to make stripes, dots, and plaids. It was a memorable day when he returned to school after a bout with measles. He headed straight for the easel during playtime and painted a large orange pumpkin-like form which he covered with brown spots. "My pumpkin is the giant of them all," he proclaimed, "and he has the measles." Whenever opportunities for painting were available, Danny was there, and his enthusiasm frequently attracted other children to join him.

The teacher's role as guide and facilitator involves more than organizing space and materials and providing time for children to use them. Teachers also recognize the importance of helping children increase their sensory awareness and encouraging spontaneity and experimentation in using art materials.

Stimulate sensory awareness

Toddlers methodically examine their environments. Discovering something new, they feel it, shake it, squeeze it, taste it, and sniff it. Their continually growing storehouse of sense impressions will affect the kind and quality of understandings they develop.

The sensorimotor mode is very much a part of the behavior of two- and three-year-old children. Knowing this, adults will be alert to the importance of young children's need to explore. Adults will provide play materials and experiences which offer children abundant sense-stimulating possibilities, such as water, sand, colored soapsuds, textured fabrics, and other art materials and processes.

Teachers of children age four and older appreciate that these children also need to be helped to experience their surroundings through sensory exploration. Increased awareness can act as a touchstone for learning, including learning through art.

Art educators have been staunch supporters of the idea that teachers need to heighten children's perceptual awareness. Linderman and Herberholz (1975) maintain that increased ability to handle visual impressions can give children a broader aesthetic base from which to relate to their world. "A more thorough immersion in sensory experiences [all of the senses] should produce deeper personal feelings that will help the child's art expression at any level (p. 36)."

In Chapter 2 Di Leo describes how young children initially perceive and represent their impressions as simple symbols. As they begin to assimilate and discriminate differences, they will include more detail in their artwork. This natural progression of development in visual perception can be enhanced by stimulation of the senses and by training for improvement of observational skills (Gaitskell 1962; Arnheim 1965; Salome 1972). The results of a study by De Porter and Kavanaugh (1978) suggest that children who receive enriched cultural and artistic experiences in their early years will have developed heightened discriminatory powers by middle childhood.

Young children need to be actively involved in the learning process. Bombardment of their sensibilities by the media does little to make them aware of differences in what they see and hear. Teachers can help children savor the richness and beauty around them. In Chapter 6 we paint a vivid picture of the importance of sense impressions in all the arts and offer some suggestions for sharpening awareness. The following techniques have also been used successfully to foster children's aesthetic growth. Why not try some?

- Arrange a shelf or corner table for things of beauty which children can admire. Contributions will gladly be offered by the parents, some of whom may have objects which represent the art of their own heritage.
- Display art prints and beautifully illustrated picture books prominently (see Appendix B). A special bulletin board called Our Art Gallery might be started.

- Collect objects which have varied aromas and place them in small containers for children to sniff and identify. Pieces of nylon stocking held in place with rubber bands make good covers. Use lemon peel, cinnamon sticks, peppermint leaves, clove, pepper, mustard, etc.
- Gather a variety of objects which have different textures, and place them in a feeling box which has a hole in the top or side that is just large enough for a child's hand to reach in and identify the objects by feel.
- Bring collections of pebbles, shells, or colored leaves for sorting by shape and color. Some children may want to share items.
- Tape-record familiar household or street sounds for children to listen to and identify.
- Have children fill various sizes and shapes of containers with different objects so they can learn to discriminate the differences in sounds when shaken.
- Take environmental walks to the same place several times for children to record changes in what they see. They may wish to adopt a tree or shrub which they can observe for seasonal changes.
- Give children an opportunity to arrange objects in an aesthetically pleasing manner—flower bouquets, fruit and vegetable centerpieces, collections of dried plants and seed pods placed in a ball of clay or block of Styrofoam.
- Visit sites that contrast with the places in which children live. For example, city children will perceive new things in a grassy park. Beaches, cornfields, farmers' markets, botanic gardens, or city streets may provide contrasts for other children.
- Allow children ages five and older to use an inexpensive camera on walks and trips. The children will zero in on things that they never would have noticed otherwise. As an introduction to photography, make small cardboard viewfinders with half-inch-square openings through which children can look to discover.
- Offer apparatus such as magnifying glasses, kaleidoscopes, prisms, and safety mirrors which will sharpen children's visual sensitivity.
- Collect magazines from which the children cut or tear pictures that can later be classified by category—foods, people, color, vehicles. The search for pictures will help sharpen perception.
- Take children on discovery walks to find patterns and textures in their environment.
- Give the children opportunities to listen to the vibrations of different sizes of rubber bands, nails, and tin cans.
- Prepare color-matching games. Color chips are free from paint stores, and yarn samples can be requested from knitting mills or stores.
- Encourage children to play active games that involve the recognition of color, shape, sound, etc. (see Kamii and DeVries 1980).
- In describing the children's artwork to them, use terms that relate to the color, form, texture, patterns, and arrangement of space.

- Be enthusiastic about your own sensory awareness and share your perceptions with the children.

What ideas can you add to this potpourri?

Encourage spontaneous response and experimentation

Unless they have previously met with repressive treatment, young children ages two through five will explore and experiment with art media, driven by a sense of curiosity about their surroundings. Children who were previously given patterns to trace or were asked to follow specific directions for artwork may take some time once again to become spontaneous with art materials. Teachers who enthusiastically accept children's discoveries and different interests can foster a spirit of exploration in the group. In addition, spontaneity can be stimulated by the kind and variety of materials made available. Children will gain a sense of what is expected of them by the way adults speak to them and by the way adults model the use of materials.

Some of the following ideas may help stimulate children's spontaneity and experimentation:

- Encourage children to try using materials in different ways if children do not discover them on their own. For example, you might say "I wonder if the back and side of the crayon will make the same kinds of marks as the pointed end."
- Exhibit sincere pleasure when a discovery is announced and share it with others in the group.
- Share your own discoveries spiritedly as you work along with the children.
- Encourage children to bring materials from home to incorporate into their art.
- Share the works of several artists which represent the same or similar theme. This will help children understand that they can draw in many different ways.
- Display the work of each child at some time during the year and call attention to the fact that everyone sees things differently (nonrealistic use of color included).
- Offer cast-offs and found materials which can be used as accessories or tools for artwork. Children will find a variety of ways to create with them. For example, they will use buttons for stringing, glued designs, wheels on toys, eyes for a puppet, or shapes for printmaking.
- Add new materials that match the group's interest at particular times. Children who live in snowy areas may need lots of white paint. Temperate spring seasons will stimulate use of pastel colors. Gold and silver papers will spark experimentation with holiday decorations. Furry fabrics will intensify interest in animals and pets.
- Make papers available in many shapes and colors. The variety will lead to more responses and experimentation with techniques.

In a supportive atmosphere, young children under six years of age will experiment with art materials enthusiastically. With the kind of encouragement we have discussed, young children will begin to create their own symbols for the world around them. Although the introduction of new materials may also spark experimentation among children over six years of age, the spontaneity of expression which we see in the art of three-, four-, and five-year-old children may begin to wane in kindergarten. Further teacher intervention may be needed to maintain spontaneity (Gaitskell and Gaitskell 1962).

In a supportive atmosphere, young children under six years of age will experiment with art materials enthusiastically.

Motivate expressiveness

Teachers can provide many experiences which will stimulate children to express their ideas visually once they are able to create symbols with art media. Sometimes little more than a group discussion will nudge children to portray an experience close to them through paint, crayon, or clay.

The day Nicole told her teacher about the new swing set her dad had installed proved to be a perfect time for the other first-grade children to take part in a discussion about their favorite play places. That afternoon several paintings of climbing and swinging apparatus were produced. These paintings were then used by the teacher to motivate interest in creating a mural about play. A trip to a space playground in a neighboring town motivated further visual expression by the children. Even David, who had just begun to create crayon symbols, drew a series of spiral-like forms and explained, "This is how dizzy I was when I went on that going-around thing."

Trips can provide excellent stimuli for children's expressiveness. Examples of oral responses inspired by a class trip to the Brooklyn Bridge are highlighted in Chapter 6. It is important, however, that the theme of any trip strike a personal chord in order for children to respond expressively. Therefore, we should not attempt to have children produce artwork on command after an excursion. Sometimes teachers can suggest art responses in an open manner, for example, "Some of you may wish to draw about the thing you liked best about our trip," or, "Before we begin to paint, let's talk about some of the things we saw on our trip." Young children will frequently become most excited about the ride on the bus or the subway and depict that part of the experience. This is perfectly fine, for what we are seeking is expressiveness.

Trips that offer children opportunities to come in active contact with people or things will stimulate the greatest interest. Thus, climbing onto the fire engine or trying on a helmet during a visit to the fire station will be most meaningful for motivating later art expression. Other places that will offer children inspiration for expressiveness are the zoo or circus, a puppet show, a pumpkin farm, a supermarket, a children's museum, or the airport. The most vivid recollections of a trip come forth within a day or two. However, some children may take time to digest the information or may need the added stimulation of related activities before they will wish to express their ideas and feelings visually.

Many teachers find that telling stories; sharing well-illustrated picture books; or showing films, filmstrips, and other media will help motivate children to create. An annotated list of some resources that can be used to stimulate sensory awareness, as well as motivate expressiveness, can be found in Appendixes A through C.

Songs and games about a particular topic can help motivate children to respond through art, especially if the topic is close to their lives. A group of second-grade children, several of whom had come from Puerto Rico, responded eagerly when the teacher joined them in singing the song "El Coqui" (tree toad). That day some of the children modeled images of the animal with clay. Others were anxious to draw "something I remember about Puerto Rico."

Bearing in mind the level of development of their pupils, teachers can choose to show appropriate reproductions of professional art as a means for motivating expression. A third-grade teacher used this technique successfully by collecting an assortment of prints representing *night* and *day* to share with the class. Some children then painted their impressions of night and day with watercolor while others used colored chalk. Because they had seen many kinds of representations, the children did not resort to stereotypes of the sun and the moon but instead mixed the colors to create shimmering impressionistic works of varied hues. This expression gave them an opportunity to reflect on past perceptions and also to practice color-mixing skills.

Many teachers of five- to eight-year-old children find that school programs that include demonstration visits by professional artists and artisans can stimulate children's creations with art materials. Sometimes resource people are drawn from among parents, thus forming a partnership between home and school for fostering art expression.

Parents who have other kinds of occupations can also visit the classroom to tell about what they do at work. A uniform or a piece of equipment the children can touch provides additional stimulus for expressive responses. It is usually not too difficult to enlist the expertise of a musician parent.

Brian's dad, an accomplished bagpipe player, had been visiting kindergarten classes yearly. When Brian was in second grade, he asked his teacher if his dad could also play for his class. Mrs. T, who had recently introduced charcoal sketching to her pupils, enthusiastically accepted the offer, for she knew this would provide another opportunity for figure sketching. In addition, she anticipated that hearing the bagpipes would also reinforce the children's knowledge about instruments and about the science of air, thus giving the experience multidimensional value. The visit was most successful. After playing the bagpipes, Mr. Sullivan willingly posed while the children made quick charcoal sketches. Their drawings were fixed with spray and attractively mounted on colored papers the next day.

Teachers can also motivate expressiveness by challenging children to solve problems through art. Many teachers ask questions that require children to use their imaginations. "How can you change the shape of the clay to make it look like something you eat?" "What parts of your hand can you use to make the finger paint look like things in the forest?" "What materials can you put together to create a puppet who could be anyone?" "How many different ways can you draw a castle?"

Young children enjoy the bizarre, the mysterious, the fantastic, and the ridiculous. When they are freed from ties to reality by suggestions the teacher makes for artwork which incorporates these themes, children will express unusual ideas and feelings. They will construct imaginary creatures with materials, draw people of the future, paint about a dream or a wish. One group of kindergarten children showed vivid imaginations in their drawings of two-headed monsters. Another group planned and constructed a foil-covered robot with an assortment of cardboard boxes.

To stimulate fluent expression, teachers use other techniques. They may ask seven- or eight-year-old children to imagine how things would look through the eyes of another being: a bird in the sky or a fish under water. A child may begin a drawing with one line and ask other children to complete it either individually or as a group. Children who are able to read can choose from a file card box of "ideas to try" collected by the teacher and children.

Recorded music can also stimulate art expression. Some teachers have children listen to music with their eyes closed and imagine moods or images. Then they draw or paint about what they have seen. Other teachers play background music to which the children's brushes dance as they paint.

In a climate of acceptance and trust such as has been described earlier in this chapter, the techniques for motivating expressiveness presented here can prove most successful.

Arrange for individual and group participation

The way children participate in art activity will depend largely on their ages. The amount of participation in art is dependent, too, on the amount of adult planning and supervision. In early childhood classrooms, the number of teachers available may influence the kind and quality of art expression.

Ideally, young children in group settings should be involved simultaneously in many self-chosen activities, some of which should involve art materials. If use of a particular medium or material requires teacher supervision, the teacher usually sits with a small group and participates in the activity with them. If another teacher or teachers are available, perhaps there will be another group activity. A teacher may wish to circulate around the room to talk to children and comment about their work. Therefore, it is unlikely there will be more than one group activity requiring close supervision.

Because two- and three-year-old children require considerable supervision, many teachers prefer to introduce or arrange for only one supervised art activity for them each day. Sometimes they will divide the whole class into small groups for simultaneous participation. Unless there are several adults, this can be a difficult undertaking. In such a setup, one-to-one interaction between teacher and child, which is so necessary in the early years, will be limited. In addition, whole-group participation in art can frequently lead to conformity of response rather than individuality of expression.

In one popular method for organizing supervised art activity, the teachers have the children take turns coming to an area where materials for art are arranged. The space will usually accommodate four to six children and provides opportunity for peer interaction as well as for interaction with the teacher. This arrangement allows for freedom of choice and gives children a chance to grow toward autonomous decision making about the kind of art they will do.

In an open classroom arrangement, which provides opportunities for movement and simultaneous participation by many pupils at several centers of interest, children four years of age and older will use art materials both individually and in small groups. Several children may be painting; a group may be using crayon or chalk; others may be cutting or pasting. Some children may also be reading books, playing in the housekeeping corner, working on teacher-assigned problems, and similar activities. When the teacher wishes to demonstrate a new art process, she may call the whole group together, and then those who wish to try the new technique will take turns that day or the next. The creative process is a personal endeavor, so most of the art work in the

early years will be done individually. After five years of age children are generally able to plan and divide work for a joint project.

The first cooperative or group art projects will usually take place in kindergarten. In most cases the children discuss the joint effort but work individually.
Then the teacher helps arrange the individual contributions into a whole. One
kindergarten teacher had been discussing types of homes with her class. The
class decided to make a mural called We All Live in Houses. Each child drew
and cut out her or his own home, and the teacher helped them arrange the
cutouts to be pasted on a large colored sheet of paper.

Another group made a lovely wall hanging on burlap about their favorite
musical story, "Peter and the Wolf." The group decided what each child
would contribute. They made characters and forest scenery with paper, fabric,
foil, yarn, and absorbent cotton. The result was a delightful group project of
which the whole class was justifiably proud.

Several kinds of group undertakings in art can be accomplished by six- to
eight-year-old children. They can take turns painting and decorating large
cartons they plan to use for dramatic play. They will design scenery backdrops
for a puppet show and create felt or burlap squares in stitchery that they can put
together into a banner about their favorite stories, pets, etc. These children can
paint murals cooperatively and decide which parts of the project they will do.
They may design and build a large construction of papier-mâché. One
second-grade class was famous for Danny the Dinosaur, which they created
over a wire frame. Some children of this age can capably write and illustrate a
story together. They may choose to place it on two rollers inside a carton for a
television-type show, or they can place the sequence of events on pages of a
booklet or accordion-folded paper. If children are given the support and respect their individual art expression deserves, they will also wish to work on
group projects with peers. They will value each other's contributions and learn
from each other as they work.

Whether art expression is done by individuals or groups, it is the teacher's
role to guide children gently in evaluating their growth as expressionists.

Evaluate children's art

Evaluation of young children's art is a delicate matter. Perhaps the term
evaluation would best be stripped of its usual connotation of criticism and be
seen in terms of *valuing*. Teachers comment on children's artwork to value
children's expressiveness, appreciate their efforts, and encourage their sensitivity to aesthetics in art.

Teachers generally act on the principle of accepting children's artwork, a
valid principle. However, to say routinely or enthusiastically to each child,
"That's beautiful," or "I like it very much," distorts the principle. Teachers
often feel uncomfortable about such blanket comments made regardless of the
artistic quality of the child's work.

How can teachers focus on the valuing and encouraging aspects of evaluation with young children? They can develop a repertoire of responses that are

encouraging and yet have integrity as they match the developmental level of the child. In some cases, no words need be spoken. A careful look at the child's work and then at the child with a smile and nod of recognition may be satisfying. With the youngest children, who are finding out what they can do with art materials, one may focus on the process. "Your brush made those long, curving free lines." "Looks like you enjoyed trying out all those colored crayons." "Oh, you were able to make all different shapes with your clay—long, skinny ones, flat ones, and these round ones." When children are at the symbolic stage in art, the teacher may occasionally (but by no means always) ask if they want to tell anything about what they have done. If children do, then the teacher has a good clue for making some relevant comment about their intentions and the processes used in their art activities.

Eventually, evaluative comments can be made to sensitize children to their work by relating what they have done to principles of art. To do this, the teacher will need to be attentive to a child's work. She may find it relevant to say something like the following: "We can tell how important the rabbit is in your collage because you have placed it near the center." "There's a nice feeling of balance in the way you used strong accents of red here, here, and here." "These repeated curves in your assemblage give it a strong sense of rhythm."

These comments refer to centers of interest, balance, and rhythm as elements in art. Other responses to children's art may relate to texture; balance in color values; or contrasts through line, color, and shape. One may also point out ingenuity in the use of materials as well as the moods expressed in children's artwork.

These types of positive evaluation generally occur after the child is finished. However, with older children ages seven and eight, the teacher may help them raise the level of their artwork through another kind of positive evaluation.

Seven-year-old Rhonda, who had a strong sense of form, was sitting back surveying her beautifully shaped clay bowl. The teacher commented appreciatively about the strong simplicity of the design as she turned the clay board completely around to better see the bowl from other angles. Sensing that Rhonda was ready to take another step in her growing technique with clay, the teacher suggested, "Let's put it up higher on this can so we can see it from a different angle." Then, with the bowl raised to eye level, they turned it slowly and could see the unevenness of the top.

"Oh, I didn't know it had those funny bumps!" exclaimed Rhonda with a tone of disappointment.

"Would you like to make it more even on top?" asked the teacher.

Unhesitatingly, Rhonda answered, "Yes." The teacher then showed her how to use a thin wire to trim the bumps without distorting the basic shape of her carefully crafted bowl. Rhonda completed the trimming, smoothed the rim, and beamed at her even more beautiful bowl. When it was dry she asked that it be displayed "up high so you can see how even it is on the top, too."

The type of evaluative intervention which the teacher used with Rhonda is quite different from the interfering type of direction to children. The teacher was helping Rhonda accomplish her own desire for improving her clay bowl. A teacher interferes when she says, "That's not finished. Take it back and fill in all the empty spaces."

There may be times when children's artwork is unusually careless, without involvement, and clearly regressive. It is not possible, then, to give an honest evaluation. At such times, the problem probably lies not with the art activity but with a more basic difficulty the child is facing and which she or he happens to reveal through art. Clearly, the teacher needs to focus on what is happening in the life of the child, not on what is being done with art materials.

Valuing and accentuating the positive aspects of a child's work are the essence of evaluation in child art.

In summary, we have pointed out several ways of evaluating the art of young children through nonverbal responses that relate to a child's intention, to the process used, and to principles of art. Such sensitive interventions can raise the levels of children's creative work. All these methods of evaluation accentuate the positive. Valuing and accentuating the positive aspects of a child's work are the essence of evaluation in child art.

References

Arnheim, R. *Art and Visual Perception*. Berkeley, Calif.: University of California Press, 1965.

De Porter, D., and Kavanaugh, R. "Parameters of Children's Sensitivity to Painting Styles." *Studies in Art Education* 20, no. 1 (1978): 43-48.

Erikson, E. H. *Childhood and Society*. New York: Norton, 1963.

Foshay, A. W. "The Creative Process and Teaching." Unpublished monograph. New York: Teachers College, Columbia University, 1961.

Gaitskell, C., and Gaitskell, M. *Art Education in the Kindergarten*. Peoria, Ill.: Charles A. Bennett, 1962.

Kamii, C., and DeVries, R. *Group Games in Early Education: Implications of Piaget's Theory*. Washington, D.C.: National Association for the Education of Young Children, 1980.

Linderman, E. W., and Herberholz, D. W. *Developing Artistic and Perceptual Awareness*. 3rd ed. Dubuque, Iowa: William C. Brown, 1975.

Lowenfeld, V., and Brittain, W. *Creative and Mental Growth*. 6th ed. New York: Macmillan, 1975.

Mendelowitz, D. *Children Are Artists*. Stanford, Calif.: Stanford University Press, 1963.

Montgomery, C. *Art for Teachers of Children*. Columbus, Ohio: Merrill, 1973.

Mukerji, R. "Creating with Children." In *Primary School Potpourri*. ed. by M. D. Cohen. Washington, D.C.: Association for Childhood Education International, 1976.

Salome, R. "Three Pilot Investigations of Perceptual Training in Four and Five Year Old Kindergarteners." *Studies in Art Education* 13, no. 2 (1972): 3-10.

4
The Art Program

When teachers understand how children develop, when we are aware of the creative process, and when we are sensitive to our role in helping children learn through art, then we have a foundation for developing the content of a good art program for young children. This chapter describes media and materials for art, plus techniques for their use. The information presented here is intended to serve as a resource bank of possibilities to which we can refer as we plan for and guide children's art expression.

Many art processes are included for children from ages two through eight to explore and use in expressing their own ideas and feelings. We hope the suggestions invite further adult/child exploration. These ideas should not be employed for step-by-step didactic teaching promoting the production of stereotyped art. Inventive teachers and children will probably discover methods for combining these materials and processes. Like professional artists, children may find that one particular process is more suitable than another. However, with the security and need to do so, children will move on to try new ways of creating visual forms.

The basic processes

Throughout history and among all cultures, three broad art process categories keep reappearing:

applying—drawing and painting, plus a variety of processes in which materials are applied to other surfaces for visual effect

forming—modeling or construction of materials into new forms, usually three-dimensional

interlacing—weaving, knotting, stitching, and twisting of natural or manufactured fibers into patterns and designs. This chapter suggests hundreds of ideas for variations of these basic processes, and also discusses simple photographic techniques.

Applying as an art process

You are probably already familiar with the basic art media children can apply to other surfaces: tempera paint, finger paint, crayons, chalk, marking pens, paper, and paste. Other items appropriate for application in a variety of ways and in different combinations are fabrics, plastics, yarn, string, glue, charcoal, watercolors, pencils, food colors, dyes, water-based inks, and natural materials. Some media can be applied directly to paper, cardboard, fabric, film, wood, and plastic surfaces. Other materials can be taped, stapled, glued, or pasted in place. All art media and materials can be used for experimental, expressive, and decorative purposes.

Painting

Two-year-old children will probably plunge into work if they are given a bucket of plain water, a wide house painter's brush, and a surface on which to paint. Add bright and beckoning colored pigment, as in water-based tempera, and the painting medium becomes particularly intriguing.

Young children respond with brushes and paint in much the same progression of stages as described in Chapter 2 for drawing. However, children's development in painting will not necessarily take place simultaneously with their development in drawing, even if given equal opportunities to use both media. Some children who have progressed from the scribble stage in drawing will keep scribbling and experimenting with paint and brushes for a while longer. While these children may be making symbols with crayon that adults recognize, they may paint only one or two brush strokes and announce, "I'm finished." Other children at the symbolic stage in drawing may use paints to fill whole sheets of paper with color, as if covering a wall.

Painting, like other forms of expression, is personal. With time and experience, most children gain the confidence and control necessary to use paint expressively. Some children will begin to make representations of people and objects, while others will use the colors to create abstract designs.

In the process of painting, children discover different techniques for using brushes. Fairly dry brushes create interesting textures; twisting a brush forms a circular pattern; and shaking the brush makes a splatter design. Children quickly find out that a wide brush works best for filling in large areas, while a thin one is useful for outlining. Accidental discoveries may also later be incorporated purposefully into paintings.

Brushes offer the most appropriate means for expression with tempera paint. Children become aware of the possible effects that can be created by painting with unconventional objects such as feathers, paint rollers, sponges, twine, cotton swabs, and paint-filled squeeze or roll-top bottles. However, gadgets such as these do not have the built-in potential of brushes for enabling children to develop symbolic expression. Therefore, painting with gadgets should not be substituted for brush painting.

The following pages contain information about tempera paint as well as the appropriate tools and accessories for children to use. Our emphasis on tempera is intended to convey its importance. Tempera is basic not only for young children, but for children all through elementary school.

Tempera paint

Tempera, an opaque, water-based medium sometimes called poster or show-card color, is available in a wide variety of hues. Children are best able to control its flow if it is the consistency of heavy cream.

Tempera paint can be purchased as a liquid, cake, or powder. To avoid the time and trouble of mixing the less-expensive tempera powder, some schools prefer to purchase economical gallon containers of the prepared liquid.

If your budget necessitates the purchase of powdered tempera, add a few drops of water to the powder and mix until a thick paste forms. Then gradually add more water to achieve the proper opaqueness and fluidity. To check, brush the paint over the print on a newspaper. The paint is just right if the type is completely concealed. Adding a tablespoon of white glue per quart will help counteract the tendency of this tempera to rub off. To further limit expenses, order only primary colors of the powder (red, yellow, blue), plus black and white. Then you can mix the other colors when required.

Oil of clove or wintergreen added in small quantities prevents liquid tempera from turning sour in storage. The addition of one-half cup of liquid laundry starch per quart also acts as a preservative. Starch acts as an extender as well and gives a smooth quality to the paint. It is easier to clean up spills if a teaspoon or two of liquid detergent is added to the daily paint supply. Tempera that contains detergent or soap will also adhere to slick surfaces. For texture effects, add small quantities of sand, sawdust, or vermiculite to the paint.

Paper for painting. Many teachers use newsprint because it is inexpensive. Newsprint tears easily, however, and can frustrate a three-year-old child who wears the paper thin by painting over and over one area. Manila and white drawing paper take tempera paint beautifully, and they are much more durable. Colored construction paper is also suitable for painting. Paper which has an interesting texture may be used when special effects are desired. Wallpaper ends, wrapping paper, shelf paper, opened paper bags, and even printed newspaper are acceptable if your budget is limited.

The most appropriate size of paper for beginners is 18 × 24 inches. The large paper offers sufficient area for the broad arm sweeps characteristic of young painters and also fits standard school easels well. Six- to eight-year-old children are able to paint on smaller paper if smaller brushes are provided.

Paper can be purchased in rolls for mural painting. It is sold in widths from 18 to 48 inches. Brown kraft paper is readily available. Rolled colored paper similar in weight to construction paper can also be obtained from art suppliers.

Brushes. Brushes with nine- or ten-inch-long natural wood handles are best for young children. If the bristles are set into seamless aluminum ferrules, the brushes will not lose hairs or rust. Very young children will manage brushes easier if you cut about two inches off the brush handles. A strip of colored tape placed around each brush handle will help beginners to replace the brushes in the matching color paint. Always store washed brushes with their bristles up.

Appropriate brush widths for two- to four-year-old children are one-half or three-fourths inches. More experienced painters can be offered brushes in a range from one-fourth to one inch wide. Children who are not limited to one size brush are more likely to experiment with different techniques.

Accessories. Containers to hold tempera paint are important. See-through plastic cups, small cans, or half-pint milk containers seem popular. If the easel comes equipped with trays, the containers can be wedged into them with wads of newspaper to avoid spilling. Containers can be wedged into small cartons or soda bottle carriers for portability.

For painting at tables or on the floor, offer children low receptacles which will not tip over, such as tuna or pet food cans, jar lids, furniture casters, and small pie tins.

If tempera is arranged in plastic squeeze bottles on an accessible shelf or counter, children ages five and older can choose their own colors and fill containers independently. Some teachers paint the tops of the bottles to match the contents. Others print the name of the color in the matching hue to aid in identification.

Easels, the traditional place at which young children paint, are also the most appropriate. Children who stand up to paint can move their arms freely and are also able to back away to survey their work at eye level. Economical substitutes for commercial easels can be constructed with Tri-Wall or wallboard (see Figure 10). Makeshift easels can be made by taping paper to walls, fences, cabinets, large cartons, and even chair backs. Young children may find it comfortable to paint at tables or sprawl and squat on the floor to paint a mural with classmates.

It may take ingenuity to find spaces and places in which children can paint, but the results will be worth the effort.

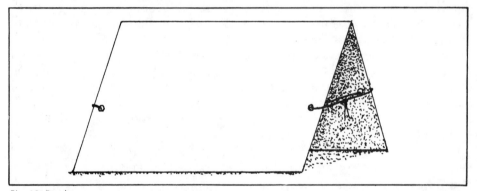

Fig. 10. Easels.

Clip clothespins, bulldog clips, masking tape, or cup hooks are helpful for fastening paper to easels and other vertical surfaces. If cup hooks are screwed into the easel, several sheets of paper can be placed on them, and the children can remove one sheet of paper at a time without adult help. Many five-year-old children are also able to place the paper on the hooks independently.

Sponges, paper towels, and fabric scraps are handy for children to use to blot excess paint or to wipe a brush which has slipped into the wrong color. Have at least one container of clear water for brush rinsing wherever painting is going on. Empty containers are needed for mixing colors; Styrofoam trays can be

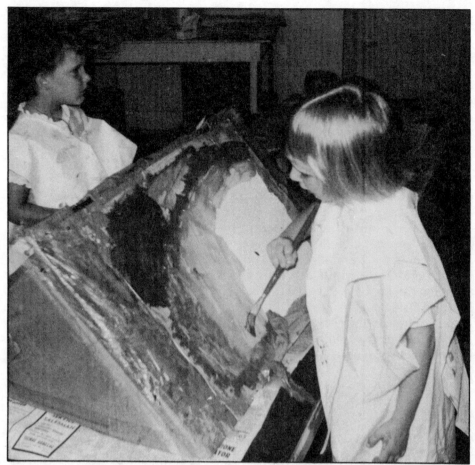

Makeshift easels can be made by taping paper to walls, fences, cabinets, large cartons, and even chair backs.

palettes for trying out new hues. If a crayon is hung on a long string at the side of the easel, children can write their names or make identifying marks on their work.

Hints. To avoid confusion, you may wish to offer only one or two colors to beginning painters. As more colors are provided, pour only small amounts of each. Then if the paint becomes muddy, it can be changed frequently with little waste.

Do not be concerned if children create drips and puddles while experimenting with paints. Children busily engaged in painting usually pay little attention to drips. When children become aware of the excess paint, they experiment with different ways of blotting it. Some children will push drips upward with a finger, and other children will blot a puddle with tissue or towels. Most children discover that wiping a brush against the inside edge of the paint cup helps prevent drips.

Watercolor

Painting with watercolor is usually not considered appropriate for young children because this thin, runny medium is difficult to control. It can, however, be used effectively by six-, seven-, and eight-year-old children who have had prior experience with tempera and may be ready for the smaller brushes required for watercolors.

Watercolors, which are sold in tube and cake form, must be thinned with water in a water cup or mixing palette before spreading. A set of moderately priced camel hair brushes in sizes 2, 4, 6, and 8 should be adequate for beginning watercolor work. Rough-textured paper, made specifically for this paint, is available in different weights, both loose and in pads. However, school-quality white drawing paper is adequate for early watercolor painting.

Watercolors can be applied as wash backgrounds for children's drawings. Special effects can be created by using the paint in different ways. A mottled look can be created if the moist color is brushed across the paper and then blotted gently with a sponge or crumpled tissue. Children can also drop puddles of desired colors and blend them, causing a marbleized appearance. The blending can be done with a brush, by tilting the paper from side to side, or by blowing on the puddles of paint. Children can also experiment with watercolor techniques by applying the paint to wet paper. Seven- and eight-year-old children, who often draw with pencils, enjoy using watercolor to fill in some areas of their lightly sketched pencil expressions.

Finger paint

Working with finger paint is a magnetic experience for most children because they enjoy its tactile stimulation, although its apparent messiness may at first upset some children. As we indicated in Chapter 3 (p. 27), a short period for observing peers at work may be all it takes to draw a reluctant child into finger painting. There are many possibilities for using this paint in addition to the traditional method in which children create designs and symbolic forms. Children can use the medium for printmaking, experiment with the colors and mix new hues, and decorate different surfaces with it. Therefore, finger paint is one of the staples of the early art program.

Types of paint. Finger paint may be purchased in ready-mixed form or in powder. The premixed, pudding-like paint is scooped out of a jar and applied to a wet surface. The powder is shaken out and manipulated on the wet surface until it dissolves. Some teachers find that the addition of a tablespoon of liquid starch helps the powdered finger paint spread well.

There are several economical methods for making finger paint. Two simple procedures follow:
1. Mix two parts of liquid laundry starch with one part powdered tempera or a few drops of food color.
2. Mix flour and cold water into a paste. Add liquid tempera or food color.
A sprinkling of soap flakes (not detergent) added to either of these homemade finger paints helps make the mixtures glide over paper. In addition, the soap

Working with finger paint is a magnetic experience for most children because they enjoy its tactile stimulation, although its apparent messiness may at first upset some children.

flakes make cleaning up more efficient. You may prefer to introduce finger painting to very young children by mixing soap flakes with a small amount of water and enough food color to make the mixture attractive.

Surfaces for finger painting. Children can finger paint on paper which has a glossy finish or on other slick, light-colored surfaces. Painting directly on laminated tables allows much-needed freedom of movement. If you do not have such tables, it may be possible to obtain scraps of laminated counter tops from kitchen cabinet manufacturers. Some teachers spread out a plain plastic tablecloth for group finger painting, or use discarded plastic window shades.

The glossy side of commercial finger paint paper takes the paint best, but glazed shelf paper is a good substitute. You may wish to roll out a long strip of this paper for several children to work together on the floor or tables, because individual papers may shift. A drop of liquid starch or a snip of double-faced tape under each corner of single sheets can also prevent slipping. If you have metal or plastic cafeteria trays, the finger paint paper may be cut to fit into them. The children paint only on the tray area. Although this method somewhat limits mobility, it makes less mess, and the trays can be stacked in alternate directions to dry the paintings.

The basic process.
1. After everyone puts on smocks, prepare a bowl of water, a sponge, and the paint.
2. Wet the surface to be painted with the sponge.
3. Use the palm of the hand(s) to spread the paint evenly over the surface, eliminating lumps.
4. Use hands, arms, fingers, knuckles, fists, fingernails (gently), and elbows to create desired effects.
5. Manipulate the paint with tongue depressors, serrated plastic knives, combs, and textured items for additional effects.
6. Add another color or colors.
7. Add a few drops of water if the paint does not glide or begins to dry.
Hint: You will need to assist very young children in lifting finger paint paper and transporting it to a drying area. If the paper curls, place it under weights or iron it between several sheets of newspaper when the paint is dry.

Printmaking

The process of applying color to objects so that their forms can be reproduced contains a surprise element which draws children to it. They frequently discover simple forms of printmaking themselves: paint-laden hands make prints as children finger paint, or they notice the sponge's image transferred to the table during cleanup.

Printmaking processes range from simple monoprints (single copies) to more complex techniques for multiple printmaking from plates or predesigned blocks. Young children engaged in printmaking learn techniques for expressing their ideas in a new art form which can also be applied later for practical purposes. In addition, children begin to understand something about the process which relates to the creation of the many symbols in the environment.

Materials and tools for printing. Thick tempera paint and finger paint are the most appropriate coloring media for early printmaking. Water-based printing inks are too difficult for children under the age of six to handle and take much too long to dry.

Children can apply color in several ways to the object to be printed. The color can be painted on with a brush, daubed on with a finger, or rolled on with a small rubber roller (brayer). A stamp pad can also be used. The method for applying color depends on the particular printmaking process.

Any surfaces on which children draw and paint can also take prints—papers, fabrics, cardboard boxes, plastic, and wood. Special art papers or delicate rice paper may be tried at special times to create interesting effects.

Monoprints. A monoprint is a single print made by pressing the paper or other surface to be printed against a painting which the child has just completed and which is still wet, for example, a finger painting on a laminated surface. Even though only one print can be made, this process gives very young children a sense of how a design can be duplicated.

Young children engaged in printmaking learn techniques for expressing their ideas in a new art form which can also be applied later for practical purposes.

With time and experience, children are able to design and reproduce fairly sophisticated splatter prints.

To reproduce a finger painting made on plastic, the child places a sheet of manila or white drawing paper gently over the paint. Next the child rubs a hand over the whole area, then picks up the paper promptly, revealing an image of the finger painting on the reverse side.

Children also create monoprints by painting a quick design with tempera paint on half of the paper and folding it over. Another type of monoprint can be produced by drawing a design or picture on a blank paper after it is placed on a table that has been coated with finger paint. If the drawing is done with a dull pencil or a ballpoint pen and a moderate amount of pressure is exerted, a colored line drawing will appear on the reverse side when the paper is lifted. Older children, who can use more pressure while drawing, may enjoy making monoprints in the same manner by picking up the color from surfaces which have been covered with crayon or chalk.

Printing with found materials. The classroom, the kitchen, and the natural environment will yield exciting materials from which prints can be produced by children. Objects such as sponges, wood scraps, erasers, bottle caps, buttons, blocks, forks, and drinking straws can be printed by using a stamp pad method with tempera paint or by applying finger paint or tempera paint to a surface with a brush or finger. Larger surfaces can be coated by using the brayer method. For this procedure, place a lump of finger paint on a smooth surface such as a tray or baking sheet. Roll the brayer back and forth in the paint until the roller is covered with a thin film of paint. Then roll the brayer over the object to be printed, covering it with color.

Very young children, whose fine muscles are still developing, can most easily use the stamp pad procedure. A homemade stamp pad can be made in one of two ways:

1. Place a flat sponge in a shallow bowl and add sufficient tempera paint to fill the sponge.
2. Make a pad from several folded paper towels. Place the pad into a shallow bowl and pour on enough paint to drench the towels.

Make certain that the stamp pad is wet enough to coat the object when the child presses down on it.

In time, children will create symbols and designs by printing with found objects. One group of seven- and eight-year-old children created a menagerie of imaginary animals by printing body parts with objects such as hair rollers, keys, Tinker Toys, spools, twine, and steel wool. Some children may combine printmaking with brush painting. Georgie had painted a "whole forest of tree trunks" at the easel. Then he used sponge prints to fill in the leafy areas with lacy brown, green, and yellow. When Maria was in first grade, she printed the buttons on her painting of a clown with a small jar lid because she wanted the buttons to be perfectly round.

Children over the age of six will find satisfaction in collecting and printing with natural objects such as leaves, grasses, tree bark, or shells. The child rolls a printing brayer onto a tray which contains finger paint. The brayer, coated with paint, is moved back and forth over the object to be printed until the object is completely covered with color. For this process, it is preferable to press the paper to be printed onto the object. The child smoothes the paper over the object's entire surface, exerting even pressure, and then pulls the paper off to reveal the print. Onionskin typing paper and rice paper receive these delicate prints well, and children are pleased by the attractive results.

Printing with stencils. Children can apply color to the area around cardboard forms, plastic shapes, and other objects so that silhouettes of the originals appear when the objects are removed. Effective stenciled designs can be created by daubing the finger paint or tempera color around the form with a brush or sponge. Splatter painting is another method used to create stencil prints. Children ages five and older can usually cut simple shapes for stencils. A collection of assorted forms can also be made from the plastic lids of coffee cans. These cutouts can be washed and reused.

For the daubing process, the child holds the shape (or tapes or staples it in place) with one hand and applies the color with the other.

Two procedures can be followed for splatter printing:

Toothbrush method
1. Place the shapes on a paper in a shallow carton. (The carton prevents children from splattering surroundings.)
2. Dip a toothbrush into tempera paint.
3. Flick the paint off the brush and into the carton by pushing the bristles of the inverted brush *toward yourself* with a fingernail or tongue depressor.

Screen method
1. Place the paper with shapes on it into the carton.
2. Cover the box with a metal or plastic screen.
3. Dip a small scrub brush lightly into tempera, then move it back and forth across the screen.

With time and experience, children are able to design and reproduce fairly sophisticated splatter prints using either of these methods.

Block printing. Children who wish to reproduce designs in quantity can use simple block printing processes by drawing their designs on plates (blocks).

Simple printing plates can be prepared from Styrofoam food trays, Plasticine, and bars of soft soap. Adhesive-backed foam sheeting can also be purchased for this purpose from art suppliers. First- and second-grade children can make more complex incised plates with balsa wood or corrugated cardboard. The plates are prepared for printing in one of two ways.
1. The design is cut away (incised) so the uncut or raised area which remains can be coated with paint (inked) and printed.
2. The parts of the design to be printed are applied to another surface of the same or another type of material as the plate. For example, cardboard designs can be cut out and glued to a cardboard plate or to wood.

To prepare and print simple incised plates:

1. Sketch the design lightly on the plate with pencil or charcoal.
2. Draw over the lines with a ballpoint pen or other blunt tool, applying enough pressure to cause the material to give, thus depressing the line (incising). Make the depressed areas broad enough so that the paint will not clog them.
3. Depress or cut away larger areas with a teaspoon or tongue depressor. A series of lines can be depressed close to one another for the same effect.
4. Ink the block's surface by moving a paint-coated brayer back and forth over the design.
5. Turn the plate over onto the surface which will receive the print when the plate is covered with color and press firmly across the entire plate. Prints can be pulled by placing printing paper on top of the plate and applying pressure to the paper.

Hint: If Plasticine is used as the block, coat it with liquid detergent so water-based paint will adhere to it.

To prepare printing plates from balsa wood, seven- and eight-year-old children can chip away areas of their designs with sharp scissors or clay-modeling tools. Children can also draw their designs on corrugated cardboard and peel away the top layer, after scoring it with sharp scissors. The exposed ridged areas then show up in the prints.

Blocks for printing can also have designs glued to them by using pieces of string, cardboard, scraps of wood, or bits of other material. If the child wishes to follow a design, it can first be drawn on the block and then the material glued over it. Thick cardboard, wallboard, scraps of wood, or small boxes make fine bases for raised blocks.

Adhesive-backed foam rubber stripping tape is another material which may be applied to a base for this process. It can be purchased in hardware stores in several widths. Try the following procedure:

1. Draw a design or picture on the base.
2. Cut snips of the tape, remove the backing, and stick the rubber to the outline of the design.
3. Ink the plate with a finger paint-coated brayer.
4. Print the design by pressing the painted plate onto the surface to be printed.

Very young children can place rubber bands on blocks of wood or rolling pins or wind twine around blocks to form crosshatched lines. These raised plates can be printed in stamp-pad fashion or in the manner described earlier.

There are many practical applications for printmaking. Children can make greeting cards, gift-wrapping paper, placemats, coasters, and any other objects which could be decorated with the same motif. One group of first-grade children decorated muslin squares with block prints and folded them into kerchiefs which they proudly wore. Another class gave their families gifts of block-printed cork sheets.

Whether printmaking with found objects or with prepared plates, children will discover new techniques and combinations. The possibilities for experimenting, designing, and producing are almost infinite.

Applying dyes

When processes such as tie and dye or batik are included in art programs, then children can come to understand about the cultures of people who traditionally use these techniques (Herberholz 1979; Fiarotta 1976). However, the processes should be simplified for young children. For example, when directions call for hot-water dye, you may be able to experiment with the process, substituting cold-water dyes such as food color. When fabric is suggested, children may try soft paper or nonwoven fabric first. Several arts and crafts books listed in Appendix C contain more detailed instructions for the simple techniques described in this section (see Wiseman 1967; Wankelman et al. 1978). Some dye manufacturers will also send free literature about the processes. You may wish to refer to these sources and try the processes yourself before introducing them to children.

Dip and dye

Three- and four-year-old children can engage in the simple but exciting process of dipping folds of paper towels or strong white paper napkins into food color baths. Through this process, children create attractive, translucent designs and also discover the magic of color mixing as the dye is absorbed into the paper.

You may wish to try the following basic procedure first and then experiment with other ways of dipping the paper or mixing the colors:
  1. Place ten drops of each color into separate cups of a muffin tin, leaving an empty section between each color so as to prevent mixing.
  2. Add one-fourth cup of water to each color and mix.
  3. Make several folds in a paper towel or napkin.
  4. Dip each corner of the folded paper into a color, allowing the paper to absorb just enough liquid so that it does not run into the next corner.
  5. Squeeze out excess liquid by pressing each corner between thumb and forefinger.
  6. Open the paper flat (with care), and place it on a pad of newspapers or towels to dry.
  7. Press the dyed paper between several thicknesses of newspaper with a warm iron for quick drying or flattening.

Hint: Children who are not yet able to fold the paper can pinch up one area at a time for dipping into the food colors.

Tie and dye

Children over the age of five can explore tie and dye techniques for decorating fabrics such as squares of unbleached muslin, handkerchiefs, and T-shirts. Use nontoxic commerical dyes that mix with water (see package instructions) or special cold-water dyes which have a food color base and are manufactured for use by children.

The patterns created by this process depend completely on the way the fabric is tied before being placed in the dye bath. When the fabric is rolled and then tied at intervals, a series of linear patterns is produced. A variety of patterns is also formed if objects such as beads, marbles, or paper clips are tied into the fabric. Part of the fun of tie and dye is the discovery of these designs and patterns.

The following procedure may be given to children initially. After some experience, other methods of tying can be tried. Because the object of this process is to keep the color from penetrating areas of the fabric which are under the string, it is important for children to tie the string securely. Those children who are unable to tie tight knots may be successful using rubber bands.

1. Prepare the dye bath in a metal or plastic tub or pail according to package instructions, so that there will be enough liquid to cover the items to be dipped.
2. Pinch together a small section of the fabric to be dyed, and wind string or a rubber band tightly around it, leaving a bubble-like knob of fabric at the end.
3. Repeat step 2 several times until the fabric is covered with tied knobs.
4. Place the tied fabric into the dye, and mix with a stick so that the color takes evenly.
5. Remove the fabric from the dye as soon as the desired depth of color is reached. Wear rubber gloves to protect hands from being dyed, too.
6. Rinse the object well with cold water, and wring it out.
7. Cut away the strings or rubber bands, and open the fabric to reveal the tie-dyed designs.
8. To use a second color, the knots can be opened, and the fabric retied in other places before being placed in the new dye bath. Dyes can be saved in closed jars for the next session or used for the batik process described next.
9. Hang the wet object to drip, and iron while damp to set the color. (Children may need assistance with this step.)

Simple batik

Children can achieve dramatic effects by modifying the traditional Indian and Indonesian batik process. The artist draws on the fabric with wax or paste and then brushes it with dye or dips it in a dye bath. Those areas of the design which were protected by the wax or paste resist the color. The wax is then removed, revealing the design. While this may sound like a simple procedure, it can become complex if the wax must be removed several times to create new designs or colors on one piece. For young children ages five and older, a one-time dye application should be sufficient to give them some exposure to the traditional method.

In both of the following methods, children can achieve the traditional crackle effect by twisting the fabric before applying dye. The twisting creates cracks in the wax or paste and allows the dye to seep into the material. For first attempts, try using scraps from an old bed sheet.

Paste method

1. Pull the fabric taut and anchor to the table or a tray with masking tape.
2. Lightly sketch the design on the fabric with charcoal. (Young children may not preplan when they try this process. Therefore, this step may be eliminated.)
3. Mix flour and water into a free-flowing paste, adding a pinch of alum.
4. Place the paste mixture into a plastic squeeze dispenser.
5. Squeeze the mixture out onto the fabric, forming the desired design.
6. Allow the paste to dry thoroughly. (This may take several hours.)
7. Brush on the dye, covering all areas without paste.
8. Chip off the paste when the dye is completely dry and reveal the design.

Hint: Young children may wish to use food colors for this process, because the intensity of the hues makes the work more attractive. The children can also use more than one color to dye the fabric.

Wax method

1. Tape the fabric taut as in the paste method, above.
2. Melt the wax in a metal container.
3. Draw the desired design as in step two of the paste method and apply one or more coats of melted wax to the design. The children may need close supervision because of the heat.
4. When the wax has set, remove the fabric and dip it into a dye bath or brush with food color as in the paste method.
5. Remove the wax by ironing the fabric between several layers of newspaper. Repeat this step, using clean newspaper, until the wax disappears.

Applying color mixtures

In the process of applying paints or dyes, children frequently discover that certain colors mix to form new hues. However, the following additional activities may be included to facilitate discovery about color.

Rollovers

For this process, one or more colors of paint are rolled onto paper, and then new colors are rolled over the wet ones to observe changes. For children under five years of age, the number of colors may be limited to two or three at a time. Red and yellow plus white, or blue and red plus white are two possibilities that will yield exciting results. Once this technique is mastered, older children should be able to select their own colors for mixing. The following materials are needed for the rollover process: 1) thick tempera or finger paint; 2) house painters' rollers or rubber brayers; 3) trays, vinyl floor tiles, shallow aluminum pans, or other flat surfaces for rolling out the paint; 4) large sheets of newsprint or other inexpensive paper. The procedure for this technique is simple: Place paint on the tray. Move roller over the paint until roller is coated. Roll the paint onto the paper.

Dribble trails

For this activity, tempera paints must be thinned with water to flow easily.

Watercolors may also be tried. A paintbrush is dipped into one color, and then the paint is squeezed from the end of the brush with the thumb and index finger so that a small puddle drops to the paper. This process is repeated with several colors. While the puddles are still fluid, another paintbrush is used to trail the dribbled paint into a maze of lines, thus blending the colors into one another.

Dropper blends

Children will be challenged to create several shades of one color if they are given plastic medicine droppers and divided cartons such as Styrofoam egg boxes or muffin tins in which to blend paint. Watercolors or thinned tempera work best for this activity. Children can use the medicine droppers to add small quantities of one color to another, increasing the number of drops put in each of the sections. For example, after putting six drops of red in each section, children can also drop varying amounts of white into each one. Children can apply the prepared shades to paper with a brush to find out which colors dry the lightest and darkest shades of pink.

Drawing

Children's pleasure in scratching designs into wet sand or on misty windows can be extended through drawing with other materials. Drawing, a technique for creating images in outline form, has long been employed by people to make symbols which communicate ideas. Young children who have passed through the kinesthetically motivated scribble stage can also begin to use drawing to convey their thoughts.

Certain materials are more suitable than others for beginners. This section will describe the kinds of tools and surfaces for drawing which best serve the developmental needs of young children.

Crayons

The term *crayon* usually refers to the common inexpensive colored wax stick, available in several thicknesses. While older children usually handle thinner crayons well, a special thicker primary size is easiest for smaller fingers to grasp. The nonroll variety (one flat side) is more economical, because it does not fall off a table or desk and break as frequently as the round type. If your budget permits purchase of an individual set of assorted colors for each child, consider the eight-to-a-box pack. The enticing array of 16 colors can be offered to kindergarten or first-grade children when there seems to be a lag in drawing activity.

When ordering in bulk, the most popular colors are purchased in the largest quantity so that replacements are available when needed. Individual assortments can be kept in each child's cubby. If like colors are placed in labeled containers, the children may learn to match colors and signs in a functional, incidental way. One method is to clip on clothespins which are painted the same color as each container's contents. In contrast, you may prefer to provide a large container of assorted crayons which children share. You may also want to include some fluorescent crayons which delight children.

While older children usually handle thinner crayons well, a special thicker primary size is easiest for smaller fingers to grasp.

Multicolored crayons can be made from bits and pieces of old ones. Remove the paper, cut the crayons into one-fourth inch bits, and warm them slightly on a sheet of aluminum foil in an oven. When the wax is of modeling consistency, quickly compress several bits into a small stick. When the wax cools and hardens you will have a multicolored crayon.

Oil crayons, sometimes called Craypas, may be more expensive than wax crayons. Their small size makes them more suitable for older children. After Craypas are applied, they can also be blended with a finger or a tissue to achieve unusual color effects. Oil crayons can be used to create vivid drawings because of their translucency and brilliance.

Paint crayons are also popular with children over five years of age. When stick colors such as Payons are dipped into water before making each stroke, the drawn lines flow almost like paint. Payons can also be used dry. After finishing drawings, children can paint over the colored areas with wet brushes to produce watercolor effects.

Types of paper. The wide variety of types of paper described in the section on tempera paint (p. 51) are also suitable for crayon work. In addition, plastic window shades, sandpaper, corrugated board, and other textured papers are particularly interesting to use with crayons.

Children frequently wish to use their drawings to decorate objects they have made from other materials. The toys and gifts they create from fabric can first be decorated with crayon. Bleached or unbleached muslin takes crayon well. The colors become more permanent if the crayoned fabric is placed between several sheets of paper and the paper is pressed with a warm iron.

Techniques. Children may discover many techniques for using crayons. Some children begin to use outline to define their drawings, while other children fill in areas with contrasting colors for accent or definition. Chris was pressing hard on her orange crayon as she drew a sun. "Look, it's the color of fire!" she announced. Other children discover that light pressure on crayons can create pastel tints. Sabrina made pastels by coloring with white on top of every shade once she discovered that the purple became lavender when she drew white buttons on her clown's purple suit.

If you work with three- or four-year-old children, remove the paper from some crayons. Encourage children to try drawing with the sides as well as tips. Older children like to remove the paper themselves. If you cut notches along the bare side of the crayons, the children can discover how to create exciting effects.

Children who are free to experiment may try drawing with two or even three crayons at once. Seven- and eight-year-old children may create multihued forms with series of dots, especially if the children are shown some of the works of Impressionist painters who used this technique. The most important consideration here is to make drawing materials available to children. Then they can choose to use them alone or in combination with other media for personal expression.

If children do not discover them, the following special effects with crayons can be demonstrated:

Scratch drawing (sgraffito) method

1. Color a small piece of cardboard or tagboard, making certain that a thick coat of wax covers the surface and that none of the paper shows. If the background paper is a light color, try using dark crayons.
2. Use a large nail, opened paper clip, or other sharp but safe tool to draw a design or picture by scratching through the crayon layer. The cardboard beneath should then be revealed.
3. Increase the complexity of this process for older children. First coat the tagboard with a layer of light color. This can be either one or several shades. A second layer of dark crayon or tempera is applied over the lighter shade. The scratch drawing is done next, revealing the light first layer.

Note: Art supply firms sell special scratchboard which comes already coated with black ink. A small, round, metal scratching tool is also available. This tool has several differently shaped notches cut into its edge.

Crayon resist method
1. Draw the design or picture on sturdy paper (not newsprint).
2. Go over all colors so that the wax layer is thick.
3. Thin a deep shade of tempera paint (black is most effective) with water.
4. Use a wide brush to paint across the whole drawing with the paint wash. Paint even strokes, one next to the other. The thinned paint does not adhere to the waxed areas but covers the background.

Hints: Try white crayon with blue paint for effective snow scenes. If clear wax candles are used, the picture then appears as the paint is applied.

Rubbings method
1. Remove paper from crayons.
2. Place newsprint, onionskin typing paper, or other fairly thin paper on top of an object or surface that has an interesting texture or raised design: coins, keys, bricks, pegboard, string, leaves, grasses, or tree bark. Another technique uses paper cutouts which can be prearranged or moved about during the rubbing process.
3. Use the *side* of a crayon, and rub back and forth over the paper in the area which covers the items to be rubbed until the desired image appears. If children have difficulty when objects shift, tape the items down.

Provide only watercolor markers for young children because the permanent type can be toxic, and the colors are difficult to remove from clothing, hands, furniture, etc.

Hints: Take the children on a walk to discover sources for rubbings. Some children may combine crayon resist with rubbings.

Rub-off stencils method
1. Draw the outline of a form on sturdy paper or tagboard.
2. Heavily crayon a border about one-half inch wide along the inside edge of the form.
3. Cut out the form.
4. Hold the cutout firmly against drawing paper, or staple it if desired.
5. Rub the color from the border onto the drawing paper using a tissue or cotton ball. Be sure to go around the entire form.
6. Remove the form. Its silhouette will appear on the background paper.

Because crayons are generally available to young children and they enjoy using them, remember that various crayon processes should not be viewed as tricks but as activities through which children gain a broader knowledge of how to produce certain effects through which their own ideas can be expressed most effectively.

Felt-tipped markers

Felt-tipped markers are sold in a wide variety of colors and in several thicknesses. Young children are able to apply even coats of color when the markers are sufficiently moist, but if the markers are too dry, the children may become discouraged and frustrated.

Provide only watercolor markers for young children because the permanent type can be toxic, and the colors are difficult to remove from clothing, hands, furniture, etc. Stains made by watercolor markers are easily removed from laminated surfaces. However, because markers easily penetrate most paper surfaces, tables and desks should be protected with newspaper or plastic.

Some manufacturers make refillable tempera paint markers for young children. Because these flat-end markers produce thick lines, children need to work with them on large paper. The smaller markers are more suitable for children to use to add detail to their drawings.

Chalk and charcoal

Colored chalk is a satisfactory medium for children as young as age three. We recommend thick sticks of the soft variety. The children can sweep the colored rods across broad areas of sidewalks, chalkboard, and paper. When chalk is used on wet paper towels, the moisture keeps the chalk dust from flying. This paper also provides an interesting surface texture.

The following techniques will help keep the powdery colors from flaking off other papers. You may wish to try all of them to see which suits your needs best. Whichever method you use, a residue of the sticky substance will eventually coat the ends of the chalk and will have to be scraped off periodically.
1. Coat the paper before drawing by brushing on a mixture of sugar and water (three tablespoons of sugar per cup of water).
2. Mix equal parts of water and liquid laundry starch and brush it onto the

paper before drawing with chalk.
3. Dip the dry chalk into one of the above solutions as you draw, instead of
    wetting the paper.

Charcoal, which is used by mature artists for sketching, can be used by
children over six years of age. As this medium is explored, children find ways
to blend lines and areas to create shades of gray. Children can pose for each
other for short periods of time during a sketching session. One group of
second-grade children was inspired to assume the postures of their favorite
athletes during such an experience. The teacher mounted and sprayed their
work with fixative, and then arranged the drawings on a bulletin board entitled
The Second-Grade Hall of Fame.

Newsprint is a good paper for beginning charcoal work. After some experience, children can draw on rough-grained paper. Charcoal pencils are better
than stick charcoal. Although more expensive, the pencils are less messy and
do not break as easily.

Pencils

Many young children wish to draw with pencils because older siblings and
adults use them. However, pencil is not recommended as a drawing medium
for children under seven years of age. Their work becomes constricted when
pencil is used. Also, the spontaneity exhibited when children draw with other
media seems to disappear if children know that pencil can be erased. Large
primary pencils may be made available to seven- and eight-year-old children
for lightly sketching work which will be completed in another medium. These
pencils do not have erasers, so work with them tends to be freer.

Other tools, other surfaces

Children can draw on many surfaces with their fingers or small sticks. For
example, pack damp sand into cafeteria trays or plastic-lined cardboard box
lids for this purpose. Children ages five and older enjoy preparing the sand
themselves. This activity is a fine introduction to the process of sand casting
(p. 89).

Drawing can also be done with white liquid glue squeezed out of plastic
dispensers. Because this glue tends to dry clear, a few drops of food color can
be mixed with the glue in the bottle. If the drawings are first sketched with
chalk, children can follow their lines with the colored glue to create an em-
bossed drawing.

Cutting, pasting, attaching

Children explore the quality of paper and other items by tearing off pieces or
snipping paper into bits with scissors. The most appropriate scissors for young
children are those with short, blunt-ended blades. The blades should be firmly
joined together for easiest cutting. Scissors can be stored in racks made for that
purpose or in inverted egg cartons with holes punched in each cup. Be sure

Children explore the quality of paper and other items by tearing off pieces or snipping paper into bits with scissors.

there are enough scissors so that children do not have to wait to use such a basic tool for their work. Children can learn to carry scissors safely by holding the blades tightly in their closed hand with the end pointing backwards.

To help children who are having difficulty in manipulating scissors, try one or more of the following techniques:

1. Provide left-handed scissors for those who need them.
2. Purchase special scissors for children whose physical handicaps prevent them from using ordinary scissors.
3. Show how to rest the bottom blade of the scissors against the edge of the table so that only the thumb needs to move to snip paper.
4. Provide narrow strips of firm, thin paper so that beginners will have success in cutting fringes or small separate pieces with single strokes.

Some young children explore paste and glue for their tactile pleasure. However, during their explorations, children can be shown how adhesives are also employed for fixing things in place.

Whether they apply found materials or create new forms by tearing or cutting, children usually begin to combine and arrange materials inventively. Children familiar with paste, glue, and other fastening devices frequently wish to use these to secure their creations.

In the following pages we describe some art processes by which children can arrange and secure papers, fabric, yarn, and other materials to create primarily two-dimensional work. Those experiences relating to the creation of three-dimensional construction or assemblages will be described in the section on forming (p. 77).

Adhesives

Water-soluble adhesives are most appropriate for young children. Library paste works best for lightweight paper or fabric. Mix your own paste with flour and water, plus a pinch of alum as a preservative. Wheat paste (wallpaper paste), purchased at a hardware store, is another inexpensive source of paste. Liquid starch and water-thinned white glue are both satisfactory adhesives for lightweight paper such as colored tissue. Glue sticks can be used for some paper, too.

Synthetic white liquid glue is the best all-purpose adhesive; it can even be added in small quantities to homemade paste to improve bonding strength. White glue can be used with fabric, wood, cardboard, and plastics. Rubber cement and contact cements are toxic and therefore not appropriate for children under the age of eight.

Thrifty teachers have found several methods for extending paste and glue supplies. These teachers give two- to four-year-old children small lumps of paste placed on jar lids, in coffee scoops, or on pieces of cardboard. Place a small quantity of liquid glue in shallow receptacles for children to share. Children age five and older are usually able to help themselves to a lump of paste from a plastic jar or bowl with a spoon or tongue depressor. If enough small squeeze bottles are available for white glue, children of this age can manipulate them independently. If only a few large bottles are available, allow children to squeeze a small amount onto a scrap of paper, and then replace the glue as it is used up.

If a damp sponge or cloth is kept nearby, children may be more willing to use their fingers for paste and glue. Paste brushes are fine, but ice cream sticks, cotton swabs, and even rolled bits of newspaper substitute well for brushes. Children frequently discover that small twigs or toothpicks are handy for applying glue to small items such as pebbles, buttons, or beads.

If children are using fine materials such as sand or gravel to sprinkle onto glued areas, put a sheet of newspaper under their work to make cleanup easier. Each color can be funneled back into its original container from the newspaper if you make a fold in the paper before placing it on the table. Be sure to clean up white glue spills while still damp. Although this substance is water soluble in its liquid state, it is difficult to remove once it is set.

Other fastening devices which children find convenient for attaching materials are tapes and gummed paper. Cellophane and masking tape are the most economical. Gummed colored paper and cloth tapes can also be used for decorative effects. Brass fasteners, staples, paper clips, rubber bands, string, and wire are also useful fasteners. Six-year-old Josh saw the potential of the brass fasteners he noticed in the teacher's desk drawer. "If I use those to fasten my circles on the black paper, I can turn the circles like the ones on the gear toy," he explained.

Much spontaneity characterizes the work of children under five years of age when they assemble and attach materials for art, while older children frequently make tentative arrangements of forms before securing them in place. The visual expressions they create by pasting, gluing, and fastening materials to each other may be nonobjective or representational. Processes children can use to express their ideas include collage, montage, and mosaics.

Collage

The term *collage* means the selection and mounting of materials on a flat surface to create a more or less two-dimensional design or picture. Collage has been used as a means of expression by serious artists; versions of it have also become a recreational pastime.

A child as young as two years of age can create a collage by pasting pieces of paper onto a sheet of cardboard or other stiff material. For beginning collage, provide children with pieces of colored construction paper, tissue in various hues, newspaper, or wallpaper. Children can cut, tear, or punch out the papers to form their own shapes. In time they will arrange both the cut-out and the cut-away parts for their creations.

Fabrics with interesting textures may be cut up and added to the collection of collage materials, along with pieces of yarn and string. Help children collect flat found materials: buttons, foils, bottle caps, cancelled stamps, and packaging materials. Leaves, shells, pebbles, and seed pods can also be combined to make attractive nature collages.

Two- and three-year-old children making their first attempts at collage often paste layers of materials on top of one another. Eventually children begin to separate the forms more, sometimes overlapping parts. This technique is particularly attractive with tissue paper because of its translucency. Children beginning to separate forms are frequently unconcerned about the messiness of oozing paste or glue. Their sense of how to apply paste neatly develops as a product of their continued experimentation. For example, one day four-year-old Calvin began a collage by spreading a large glob of paste on a sheet of cardboard. Then he tore a piece of wallpaper into smaller bits. As he started to apply the wallpaper to the cardboard, he discovered that some wallpaper did not stick to the cardboard. He spread another lump of paste over a fairly large area of his cardboard base. By the time he was down to his last few pieces of wallpaper, this paste had dried, too. In a determined manner, Calvin placed a small bit of paste on each of the remaining papers and pressed them onto his collage. In his later collages, Calvin applied paste to individual objects to secure them in place.

Pasting a collage with layers of tissue paper is particularly attractive because of the paper's translucency. Small amounts of glue can be placed on a shallow receptacle to prevent waste.

Experienced pasters combine several kinds of items in their collages. If a variety of materials is available, children may find some appropriate for adding to their drawings or paintings.

Melted crayon

This process is actually a form of collage which uses melted wax as the adhesive instead of paste or glue. It is recommended, with supervision, for children over the age of five because heat is used.

Drawing-paper method

1. Shave pieces of old crayons into bits with a plastic grate or the edge of dull scissors.

2. Arrange the crayon shavings into a design or picture on a sheet of drawing paper.
3. Cover with a few sheets of unprinted newsprint.
4. Press with a warm iron until the crayon sticks to the drawing paper. (It need not be melted flat.)

Waxed-paper method
1. Shave crayons as described earlier, and arrange them on a sheet of waxed paper.
2. Add bits of colored paper, cellophane, leaves, or string.
3. Cover with another sheet of waxed paper and a newspaper for padding.
4. Press with a warm iron until the two pieces of waxed paper stick together, securing the collage.
5. Trim the waxed paper, and display the collage on a window or suspend it on a string so that light shines through.

Montage

The steps in assembling a montage are similar to those for creating a collage. However, the montage process uses only elements from ready-made pictures. Parts of photographs, magazine illustrations, or pictures from catalogs are assembled and pasted to create new images. A group of seven-year-old children created surrealistic montages of bizarre characters using magazine illustrations of fruits for eyes and chimneys, green beans, or spaghetti for legs. Whether children's montage creations are abstract or pictorial, the opportunity to engage in this process certainly can provide an outlet for imagery.

Mosaics

Traditionally, mosaics are created by arranging cut glass or ceramic tiles (tesserae) in a wet cement or plaster compound. However, many adaptations of this process can be accomplished by substituting other materials for the tiles, such as squares of construction paper, pebbles, buttons, bits of dyed egg shell, and bottle caps. Sliced crayons, small sea shells, seeds, and colored gravel can also be used. These substitutes are glued or pasted on the surface to be decorated, and, as in montage, the designs thus formed may be either abstract or representational.

The process of creating a mosaic design involves four essential steps:
1. Draw the design on the base.
2. Separate the areas which will receive different colors and mark edges with crayon lines or glued-on string.
3. Spread glue on one area.
4. Apply the tesserae to fill in that area.
5. Repeat steps 3 and 4 until the entire design is covered. To simulate real mosaics, leave small spaces between the glued-on items. Shake off loose items such as gravel or eggshells and replace them in their original containers before starting new areas.

Yarn painting

The popular Mexican process of gluing yarn designs on flat surfaces is a suitable creative art activity for young children. In its simplest form, the child draws a linear pattern with glue and places a piece of heavy yarn such as roving or rug yarn on the glue. Children ready for more complexity can sketch the form with chalk, follow the chalk line with glue, and then apply the yarn. The more yarn to be applied, the stiffer the base needs to be. For example, if the design the child draws will be filled in with yarn, it may be well to use Masonite or plywood as a base. Five- and six-year-old children should have no difficulty

Young children use two techniques when they create symbols with clay. Many children pull out parts from the original lump of clay. Others add pieces of clay to one another.

creating outline yarn paintings. Older children can fill in each area of their designs with concentric rows of yarn.

Forming as an art process

Young children playing with mud, sand, and water frequently begin by modeling pies and later forming intricate castles (see Hill 1977). At home, while cookie dough or pie crust is being prepared, children might ask to play with some. Children also spontaneously create three-dimensional assemblages with found objects. Children pile mud, shells, sticks, and pebbles on top of one another and collect boxes, cans, and other cast-offs to construct new forms.

In planning early art programs, consider children's natural interest in creating three-dimensional forms to model, assemble, construct, cast, and carve. Those substances whose form can be easily changed are most appealing and appropriate for very young children. Modeling media such as clay or dough clay; paper which can be cut, torn, bent, and folded with little effort; soft wire and lumber; and Styrofoam and other compositions are among the most popular. Found objects, both natural and manufactured, also lend themselves well to children's early attempts at forming. Primary-grade children can also use plaster, papier-mâché, sawdust, and casting compounds for three-dimensional art work.

Modeling

Clay

Moist clay is the most appropriate modeling medium for children. Its responsive quality and pleasant feel draw them to explore many ways of forming clay. During the initial manipulative stage, children will squeeze, pinch, pat, pound, pull, and roll this soft, water-based substance. Because clay is so malleable, children soon discover how simple it is to make a direct statement with it. Although hands are the best tools, children may use tongue depressors or ice cream sticks to create special effects, but only after they have explored the clay with hands and fingers. Children need to learn housekeeping rules, but children under five years of age need few other instructions for working with clay. Older children who are ready to produce specific representations may need guidance similar to that recommended on page 26.

Young children use two basic techniques when they begin to create symbols with clay. Many children will pull out parts from the original lump of clay. Other children add pieces of clay to one another. Those who use this additive method may become frustrated when the water in the clay evaporates, causing the pieces to shrink and separate. A simple method for making clay pieces adhere to each other is to scratch (score) the two surfaces to be joined with a pencil or stick. Dilute a small lump of clay until it looks like thick glue (called slip) and place this semiliquid between the two scored surfaces. Press the pieces of clay together firmly and smooth the joined area.

Care and preparation of clay. You are fortunate to have a constant source of modeling material if the soil where you live contains natural clay. If you must purchase clay, choose from among several varieties. Self-hardening (not to be fired) clay can be obtained in five-pound boxes from art and early education materials vendors. Potter's clay, which can be fired as well as air dried, is less expensive but must be purchased in a larger quantity. This gray, buff, or terra cotta clay is sold in moist or dry powdered form. If you prefer to constitute your own clay by mixing the powder with water, make just enough for immediate use and avoid the tedious process of reconstituting when prepared clay becomes dry from exposure to the air.

To keep clay at the proper consistency, store it in air-tight child-accessible containers such as heavy trash bags or covered plastic garbage pails. Thin wire or fishing line may be used to cut a large block of clay into conveniently sized lumps of about one-half pound each. If the lumps of clay are to be stored for some time, they will have to be kept moist. Depress a small area on each piece with your thumb to create a water well. Before closing the container, place water into each depression. A moist sponge or wet cloth in the container keeps clay workable for short periods of time. A good test for checking the workability of clay is to roll a small lump into a snake-like coil and wrap it around your finger. If the clay remains smooth and does not crack, the moisture level is right. Children ages five and older can assist in caring for the clay by forming it into fist-size balls and making the water depressions. One or two children may be designated as clay helpers to close containers each day at cleanup time.

Working with clay
1. Work on washable surfaces. Plastic sheeting can be used to protect nonwashable surfaces.
2. Use clay boards made of smooth Masonite or plywood on tables. Work in progress can be moved on the boards at cleanup time.
3. Cover work in progress with a plastic bag to keep the clay soft.
4. Remove finished pieces from work surfaces by running a length of wire or fishing line under the clay and pulling it through.
5. Keep a small pan of water on the clay table so that children can moisten fingertips to smooth cracks in the clay.
6. Roll out too moist clay to dry on an absorbent surface such as a plaster of paris slab (bat) or on ceiling tile to absorb water.
7. Have children pick up small bits of clay by pressing a larger lump onto them.
8. Check shoe soles to avoid having children track clay that has dropped on the floor.
9. Wipe tables with sponges, then remove additional clay with a dry cloth.
10. Save children's clay work by leaving it exposed to the air to dry.
    Note: Clay work by young children need not be fired or finished in any way. It is attractive in its natural state, although some teachers may wish to have children brush on clear shellac to simulate the gloss of glaze.

Clear acrylic spray may be applied only in a well-ventilated area. Appendix F contains sources on finishing procedures such as firing and glazing.

11. If dry pieces of clay accumulate, pulverize and reconstitute them after removing foreign substances.

After children have manipulated the clay and discovered their own techniques, you may wish to show them some of the following pottery-making techniques. These simple directions for pottery are only a beginning. Explore clay work yourself by enrolling in a class and referring to the resources in Appendix F.

Pinch pots
1. Roll clay into a ball.
2. Press your index finger, dowel stick, or a pencil into the ball.
3. Rotate the clay while pressing against the depression with finger or stick, thus widening the depression.
4. Pinch the walls of the pot with your thumb and index finger until the sides of the pot are of the desired thickness. Walls that are too thin will collapse.
5. Rotate your work to check symmetry.
6. Smooth surfaces with moistened fingers.

Slabs
1. Place a lump of clay between two sticks as thick as you wish to make the slab (one-half or one-fourth inch) (Figure 11).
2. Roll the clay flat with a rolling pin. Trim the slab to its desired shape with a pointed stick.
3. Decorate the slab by finding items that will create interesting textures. Press combs, fork tines, wire mesh, burlap, sticks, and other items onto the surface of the clay.
4. Form a box by joining several slabs together using the scoring and slip method described on page 77.
5. Drape a slab of moist clay over a bowl or suspend it in a cloth to form a pot.

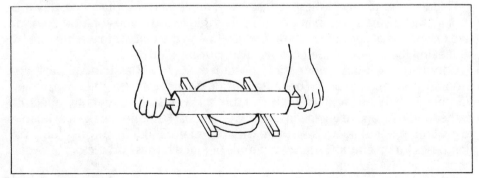

Fig. 11. Clay slab between sticks.

Coiling
1. The sides of a pot can be built up by layering coils of clay atop one another. In addition to the scoring and slip method, extra clay may be added on the inside surface of the pot to join the layers. Smooth the clay in between the coils.
2. Either a slab or coiled base may be used for the coil pot. However, the coils for the base should be thicker than those for the side walls. Different shapes can be achieved by varying the lengths of the coils as the side walls are built.

Other modeling materials

If natural clay is unavailable, **homemade modeling compounds,** which are next in suitability for very young children, may be substituted. Be sensitive, however, to the fact that the world's food supplies are limited and should be used sparingly, if at all, for non-nutritive purposes.

Children will enjoy preparing these homemade clays, which can be colored or used in their natural state. Store them in the refrigerator to extend their life.

Self-hardening dough clay (baker's clay)

1½ c. salt	Mix the dry ingredients together in a plastic bowl, then
4 c. flour	add the water gradually. When it forms a ball around the
1½ c. water	spoon, knead the dough well, adding water if it is too
1 tsp. alum (as preservative	crumbly. This clay can also be baked.
when clay is not baked)	

Soft dough clay (nonhardening)

Follow the previous recipe but add one-half cup cooking oil and reduce the amount of water to one cup.

Cornstarch clay (hardens to a smooth finish)

1 c. water	Mix the water and salt and place the pan over medium
3 c. salt	heat. Gradually mix in the cornstarch and heat until the
1 c. cornstarch	mixture thickens into a mass. Cool the clay on a piece of
	aluminum foil before kneading.

To add color to any of these recipes with the least mess, place the clay in a strong plastic bag. Drop in approximately three to four drops of food color or two teaspoons of tempera per cup of clay. Knead the color into the mixture by squeezing the bag until the color is evenly distributed.

Commercial oil-based modeling substances such as **Plasticine** are less appropriate for young children because they do not have the flexibility necessary for children's hands and strength. Temperature changes frequently affect its malleability. If you are given Plasticine with your art supplies, make it available to the children, but do not substitute it for real clay. Children may use lumps of it as bases for assembling found materials or place bits as connectors between parts of a construction.

If the Plasticine is of good quality, six- to eight-year-old children may model more sophisticated figures with it. To paint Plasticine, add liquid detergent to the paint or wipe the paintbrush against a bar of soap before applying paint.

Children with well-developed hand and finger coordination are able to model with other mixtures which, when dry, can be used for puppet heads and other sculpture. **Paper pulp** mixtures made for this purpose are available from art supply dealers. When mixed with water, these materials form a mash with shredded newspaper. Tear the paper into very small bits, add water, and boil it to a pulp, mixing continually. Add wheat paste gradually until the mixture is malleable. Oil of clove or wintergreen can be added as a preservative if the pulp is to be stored.

Another modeling medium which older children can prepare is **sawdust clay.** One cup of strained sawdust is mixed with one-half cup of wheat paste and one-half cup of water. A tablespoon each of plaster of paris powder and white glue may be added to increase bonding. If more water or wheat paste is needed to make the clay workable, add it gradually.

Children creating characters from pulp or sawdust clay can insert found items for facial features while the work is still wet. To make a puppet head, the modeling mixture may be applied at the top of a cardboard tube. The tube then becomes the puppet's neck. Both paper pulp and sawdust clay take several days to dry, so turn the work frequently for air to circulate around it. To keep pressure off soft, delicate parts, place the work in a cradle of crumpled newspaper during the drying process. The dry sawdust clay can be sanded lightly and then painted. Both paper pulp and sawdust clay take paint well. For additional durability, coat items with shellac or clear nail polish.

Constructing

Paper

Paper is one of the staples of early childhood art programs because of its versatility. In the section related to pasting and attaching (p. 70), we described several ways to create two-dimensional expressions with this medium. Flat paper may also be formed into three-dimensional structures by folding, twisting, curling, coiling, pleating, scoring, incising, wadding, or rolling. Even when three-dimensional constructions are made primarily of other materials, paper can be used to decorate them.

Young children find many ways to use paper in constructions. Children can roll paper strips tightly around a crayon and use the resulting springy curls as hair and eyelashes to complete constructions of people and animals. A useful fan is created by folding paper back and forth into pleats. Some children find that the fan shapes can also be attached as fins to paper fish or as tails to birds. Karen found that she could make a relief sculpture when she pulled up the loops of her woven paper mat to make hills. Tricia piled up several rings she had made from gummed paper and then secured them methodically with tape. Her colorful ring sculpture received many accolades from her peers.

Paper can be crumpled and glued to other surfaces for textured effects.

When heavy paper is scored (cut through partially with pointed scissors), it can be folded easily. Folded paper can also be cut in many ways for decorative structures. A diagonal cut into a fold can be bent open when the paper is flat, revealing a triangular shape. A series of such cuts creates a relief sculpture on a flat surface. A process called quilling uses coils of paper assembled to create designs and symbols of objects such as flowers and birds. Arts and crafts instruction books are replete with descriptions of other processes for constructing with paper (see especially Kampmann 1967 and Munson 1970 in Appendix F).

Our discussion is limited in order of complexity to three paper construction processes that young children can handle successfully.

Wadded paper.
1. Crumple a small sheet of newspaper into a wad and stuff it into a sturdy lunch-size paper bag.
2. Repeat the first step until the bag is filled and a compact form has been achieved.
3. Close the open end of the bag with staples, rubber bands, tape, or pipe cleaners.
4. Dip the stuffed bag into wheat paste so it will dry stiff and be easy to paint.
5. Paint the bag with bright tempera colors.
Note: These are instructions for the basic form. Three-year-old children can make these for toss toys. Older children may prefer to add a head and limbs or cut paper to create an animal or human form.

Tube construction.
1. Cut colored construction paper into strips of several lengths and widths, such as two-, four-, and six-inch-wide strips which are four-, six-, and eight-inches long.
2. Roll each strip into a tube, overlap the edges, and fasten with tape.
3. Arrange the rolls on top of one another or next to each other to create a pleasing structure.
4. Turn the tubes so that the tape is concealed and glue them to each other with white glue.
Note: Cardboard tubes which come from many household products can be painted or covered with construction paper and assembled in similar fashion.

Papier-mâché—regular process. Durable toys and decorative objects can be created inexpensively with papier-mâché. Essentially, the process consists of covering an object with layers of paste-coated paper strips and allowing them to dry and become a hard shell. Sometimes the base form is removed, for example when a plastic bowl is covered to create a mâché bowl. At times, a complete object is covered with the paper strips. To remove the object, the dry mâché shell is cut in half, and the form is taped together again and painted. This process is necessary when a puppet head is made over sculptured Plasticine or when fruits are molded directly over the real thing.

This is the basic procedure for papier-mâché:
1. Tear newspaper or paper towels into many strips approximately 1 × 3 inches in size.
2. Prepare wheat paste in a plastic bowl according to package directions.
3. If the base form is to be removed, coat it with petroleum jelly (optional).
4. Dip a strip of paper into the paste mixture, coating it thoroughly on both sides.
5. Squeeze the strip between thumb and index finger to remove excess paste.
6. Place the strip on the base form, and repeat with other strips until the form is completely covered with two or three layers of *overlapping,* paste-coated strips.
7. Allow each layer to dry before beginning the next. If this is not convenient, be certain that each layer has strips going in different directions and not directly over each other.
8. Paint dry mâché form with tempera.
9. Shellac can be applied for additional protection and an attractive sheen.

Children can cover an inverted aluminum pie pan coated with petroleum jelly to create a simple mask. If children coat a balloon with several layers of paste-coated strips, the mâché form can be used as the head for a large figure. Children paint the papier-mâché shells with tempera and then find many innovative ways of decorating with glued-on accessories. Seven- and eight-year-old children can fashion puppet heads by covering balls of wadded newspaper with papier-mâché. Cover the wadded paper balls with sheets of tissue and tape them to cardboard tubes for necks. The tubes also serve as convenient handles while working on the puppets.

Papier-Mâché—quick method (lamination). Young children enjoy this process because instant success is assured. In describing it to them, you can compare it to buttered paper.
1. Smear three or four large sheets of paper with paste and secure them to each other. (A sheet of drawing paper on top and bottom and two sheets of newspaper between work fine.)
2. Place the moist paper sandwich on an inverted bowl, secure it with a rubber band, trim while moist, and allow to dry in the form of the bowl.
3. When dry, paint the paper bowl.

Children can produce a set of inexpensive china for the housekeeping area. A moist paper sandwich can also be cut into a variety of free-form shapes which are molded into three-dimensional forms while wet. When the shapes are dry, apply paint and string them into a necklace.

Found materials
Children who favor expressing their ideas and feelings in three-dimensional form inventively assemble cast-offs. Help them collect cardboard boxes and tubes, Styrofoam and wood scraps, egg cartons, discarded jewelry, and other useful materials such as those listed on page 34. Once the cast-offs are col-

Children who favor expressing their ideas and feelings in three-dimensional form inventively assemble cast-offs.

lected, the child chooses a base on which to build.

A base is essential to any found-materials assemblage or construction. Modeling media can be used as the base material on which to build assemblages. Children poke ice cream sticks, straws, toothpicks, and pipe cleaners into a lump of soft clay, sometimes adding beads or bits of colored paper. One day four-year-old Kelly found a box of Styrofoam packing discs. He stuck one disc on each of several toothpicks, then pushed the toothpicks into a mound of dough clay, creating a landscape of mushroom-like forms.

Other materials which can be used as bases are cardboard, ceiling tiles, small cartons, pieces of Styrofoam or wallboard, blocks of wood, and sand- or plaster-filled cans.

Materials which are used for constructing assemblages can be fastened to bases in a variety of ways. The suggestions in the section on pasting and attaching (p. 30) may prove helpful. Children usually find ingenious ways of solving the problem of how to attach materials. On the day that six-year-old Carla was having difficulty making pipe cleaners stand upright on a block of wood, she found her solution at the woodworking bench. Carla hammered a large nail into the wood, pulled it out, and hammered it in again. She repeated this process several times in different spots on the wood block. Then she cleverly placed glue in each of the nail holes, inserted a pipe cleaner in each hole, and proudly displayed her solution to her real problem. Other solutions for fastening assemblages to bases include using U-staples to secure wire to wood bases, connecting elements of a construction with string and yarn, and fastening with wire twist ties.

A three-dimensional construction with a base resting on a horizontal surface is usually called a **stabile,** or assemblage. An assemblage which is suspended, or whose parts are suspended, is called a **mobile.** True mobiles are too difficult for young children to make because the elements must be in delicate balance to move around each other. However, children may enjoy simulating mobiles by suspending cutouts and other items from wire hangers, paper plates, or dowel sticks.

Interesting effects can be created when assemblages are made of interlocking parts. Squares and rectangles can be cut from Styrofoam supermarket trays or shirt cardboards. The child cuts a slit halfway across one piece and then locks it on to another which has been slit in the same way. The pieces of Styrofoam or cardboard are built higher and wider until the desired structure is completed. A drop of white glue can be placed at each connection to secure the structure.

Many children assemble found materials to build things related to specific themes such as unusual characters, vehicles, or buildings. By engaging in this simple construction, children see relationships between various forms and learn to recognize the potential of different materials. One kindergarten group made Creatures and Cars, and some first graders built Skyscrapers and Astronauts. These creations were made of cereal boxes, egg cartons, and cardboard tubes which were attached to each other with masking tape. Once the constructions were attached, the children covered the entire forms with a layer of paper towel papier-mâché. The children painted their work with tempera when it was dry and later glued on embellishments such as feathers, curtain rings, rhinestones, and pipe cleaners.

Constructions made with large appliance cartons are also appealing. Children who build structures such as caves, cars, trains, robots, and puppet theaters for dramatic play gain the opportunity to explore and arrange space and form—important experiences for their development. If you help them (when necessary) cut out parts of or join pieces of these structures, the children will paint, decorate, and use them with zeal.

Woodwork

Have you made the acquaintance of the manager of a local lumberyard or carpentry shop who can provide you with a continuous supply of scrap wood for your art program? You might also arrange a trip to a lumberyard with the children to pick up a bundle of scraps. You may also need to purchase bags of wood turnings and other scraps sold by craft supply dealers.

Making an assemblage of scrap wood is a good introduction to woodwork. A tub containing small pieces of soft wood such as pine, spruce, or bass can be made available to the children, along with other materials for assemblage. Include wooden buttons, pieces of molding, scrap turnings, furring strips, bits of doweling, ice cream sticks, and wooden coffee stirrers.

An assortment of fine- to coarse-grained sandpaper (the smaller the number, the finer) should be included with your supplies for wood assemblage. Wrap several small blocks with different sheets of sandpaper and staple or tack the paper in place to make easy-to-handle sanding blocks.

Allow the children to manipulate the wood and sandpaper before gluing the assemblages. In the course of their experimenting, children should discover how sandpaper smooths rough lumber. You can demonstrate how rubbing *with* the grain will not scratch the way sanding *across* the wood grain does. After learning how to prepare the wood scraps, children can use white glue to create assemblages. For individual work, a small block of wood or a discarded cigar box makes an excellent base. Groups of four- and five-year-old children eagerly participate in creating assemblages together when the teacher provides large planks for bases.

You will be opening the door for many additional creative experiences if you can provide a place for children to work with lumber. Children as young as age three, who are properly supervised and know the safety rules, can participate in a full woodworking program of sawing, nailing, and drilling, as well as sanding and gluing. The opportunity to hammer one nail into two crossed strips of wood to create an airplane is not difficult to arrange. If you learn the simple rules for using a crosscut saw and hand drill, you will have the confidence to share these tools with children. Of course, a workbench with a vise is useful. An old desk or table is a fine substitute if the height is comfortable and C-clamps are available to hold the wood while the children work. The following ideas for woodworking should help you get started:

1. Place the workbench or worktable away from busy traffic flow areas.
2. Provide sturdy adult carpentry tools, not toys.
3. Establish safety rules with the children regarding numbers allowed to work together, proper use of tools, and responsibilities for cleanup.
4. Provide large nails (two to three inches long) with large heads for beginners.
5. Allow ample time for pounding.
6. Cut an old broomstick into thin discs which children can use for wheels.
7. Provide a broom and dustpan for cleanup.

Children who build structures such as caves, cars, trains, robots, and puppet theaters for dramatic play gain the opportunity to explore and arrange space and form—important experiences for their development.

8. Paint the shape of each tool on a pegboard which is within the reach of the children, so that cleanup becomes a matching game.

9. Add screwdrivers, screws, hinges, screw eyes, hooks, glue, rulers, and thick-leaded pencils as the children appear ready to use them.

10. Make tempera, felt markers, and shellac available for finishing. Wood stains may be offered to older children. Because natural wood has a beauty of its own, do not be concerned if wood assemblages are left unfinished.

Casting and carving

While it is generally true that young children discover techniques for using materials during the creative process, methods for creating forms with certain materials may need to be demonstrated. Processes with several steps or requiring particular skills fall in this category. They are mostly appropriate for children over five years of age. Papier-mâché (p. 82) is one such process. Casting and carving are others.

Plaster

Plaster of paris is an inexpensive medium that children can use to cast three-dimensional forms. Although more durable casting compounds may be purchased, plaster is an exciting, responsive medium which beginners can try for expressive, decorative, and functional purposes. Children mix the plaster according to package instructions and then drop spoonfuls onto waxed paper, thus creating abstract-shaped globs. The forms created lend themselves well to decoration with paint or markers as pendants or pins.

Mixed plaster can also be cast in molds such as waxed cartons which are torn off and discarded once the plaster sets. Plaster can be used to cast designs drawn in wet sand or Plasticine. Found objects can be arranged in sand and then cast in plaster to make attractive wall plaques or paperweights.

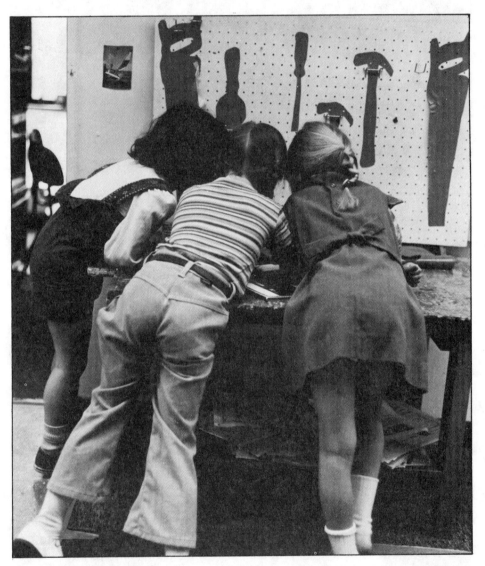

Groups of four- and five-year-old children eagerly participate in creating assemblages together when the teacher provides large planks for bases.

If you are planning to demonstrate plaster casting to children, it may be helpful to review the following general procedures:
1. Protect work surfaces with newspaper or plastic cloths.
2. Grease with petroleum jelly or lightly oil any mold which will be reused.
3. Use a pliable bowl for mixing so that leftover plaster can be peeled away when set.
4. Follow the mixing directions on the package, always sifting the powder *into* the water and working out lumps with fingers. The plaster should look and flow like thinned sour cream when it is ready to pour.
5. Work quickly because plaster sets in a short time.
6. Set hooks (paper clips work well) for hanging, or pierce holes for threading, while plaster is still soft.
7. Throw waste into the trash, *not into sinks,* because plaster clogs drains.

Sand casting. This process can be done at the beach or in outdoor sandbox areas to avoid some of the mess that working indoors with plaster may entail.
1. Pack damp sand one inch thick into a smooth area the size of the desired cast, building sand walls at least two inches high around the edges. If work is done indoors, use a cardboard box lid (greased or lined with plastic) to hold the sand, making sure the lid is more than two inches deep.
2. Using a finger or stick, make a line drawing in the sand.
3. Mix the plaster and pour it into the mold so that it covers the drawing and is at least one inch thick.
4. Allow the plaster to set until it is hard and cool.
5. Remove the cast and brush off excess sand. You may rinse it quickly with water if you like, but handle it gently and allow it to dry once more.
6. Try the same process, but substitute shells, pebbles, and other found objects for the drawing, or press them into the sand around the drawing. Leave these objects in the sand to become part of the cast, or press them into the sand and remove them, leaving impressions of their forms. Be sure to reverse any lettering which is to be part of the sand cast.

Plasticine impression molds. The method for creating castings with Plasticine is similar to that for working in sand. Be certain, however, that the clay is soft enough to receive impressions.
1. Roll out a one-inch thick slab of Plasticine as described on p. 79.
2. Trim the slab to the desired size.
3. Draw the design or picture with a blunt stick or ballpoint pen, or make impressions of found objects. Avoid making undercut lines when drawing in the Plasticine by holding the drawing tool upright. If there are no undercut areas into which the plaster can flow, the clay can be pulled away quite easily.
4. Build a two-inch or higher wall around the Plasticine with strips of cardboard. Be sure to secure any seams with masking tape to avoid leaks.

5. Grease the inside of the cardboard.
6. Mix the plaster and complete the cast as for sand casting.
7. To cast a form which will have a small hole in it for stringing, insert a plastic drinking straw, holding it upright in the mold, while the plaster is poured around it. Other greased forms may be held in the mold to create larger holes in cast blocks.
8. Pull away the cardboard and Plasticine after the plaster has set.

Casting in waste molds. Collect paper cups, milk cartons, yogurt and cottage cheese containers to use for preparing plaster blocks for carving or assembling. Remind children to grease any mold they want to use again. Most molds can be discarded, however, for it is easy to rip them off once the cast sets. Encourage the children to use the general casting method, and to pour blocks of different sizes and thicknesses. Because plaster breaks easily, suggest that blocks for carving be made at least two inches thick.

Once plaster blocks have been cast, the children can scratch designs on the surfaces. Ice cream sticks or scissors are used to trim edges, modify shapes, and carve out depressions. The starkness of white abstract forms is quite attractive in itself. However, tempera paint, markers, and colored nail polish may be used to decorate carvings. An antique finish can be produced by rubbing a bit of black or brown wax shoe polish on the plaster carving.

Gauze casting. Plaster-impregnated gauze can also be used to cast forms. A special gauze, sold under the name Pariscraft, is cut into small pieces, dipped in water, and applied to a form, as are the strips in papier-mâché. Children can prepare forms to be covered with the strips by wadding newspaper and securing its shape with masking tape. Cardboard additions or other objects can be taped onto the newspaper. For example, add ears, snouts, and horns of puppets before the gauze strips are applied. Another type of armature (base form) to cover with Pariscraft can be made with soft wire. The wire ends are stapled to a block of wood, or imbedded in plaster in a small can. The wire is then bent into the desired form and covered with strips of gauze or plaster. The wet plaster on the gauze hardens quickly and if the gauze strips are overlapped well, only one layer will be needed to cover either the newspaper or wire form. The gauze-covered piece looks and feels like cast plaster and can be decorated in the same fashion. A coat of shellac will give the piece added protection from moisture.

Other materials

Materials such as cast paraffin, soft soap, or commercial carving substances are sometimes given to older children for carving because their manual dexterity has been developed and refined. We do not recommend their use for children under the age of eight.

Puppets and masks

Sometimes the process of forming results in the creation of a functional product. Children may create bowls from clay, toys from wood, or gifts from a variety of materials. Two additional forming processes which result in functional products are puppet and mask making.

Puppets

Although some of the previously described processes might be used by children over five years of age to form puppet heads (papier-mâché, sawdust modeling, and Pariscraft), this section will be devoted to suggestions about the kinds of puppets children can create even at age three. For more detailed information about making puppets, refer to books listed in Appendix C.

Stick puppets. To make a stick puppet, the child draws a figure on paper, cuts it out, and attaches it to a tongue depressor or other handle. The figure can be dressed with fabric appliqué or a paper suit, or decorated with paint or crayon. A simple stick puppet can also be created from a wooden spoon. The child places the facial features on the back of the spoon, glues on hair, and prepares whatever clothes are desired. For example, cloth which has a small hole in its middle may be used as a gown. Push the tip of the spoon handle through the hole, pull the fabric up under the bowl of the spoon, and attach it with tape or a rubber band.

Wooden clothespins can also be made into stick puppets. A clothespin can be painted and clothed with glued-on found accessories such as felt, yarn, gummed paper, and small beads. A twisted pipe cleaner may be added for arms and an ice cream stick or tongue depressor then glued to the clothespin as a handle.

Tube puppets. Cardboard tubes, which come in several sizes, are simple for young children to turn into puppet characters. They can be painted, crayoned, or dressed with fabric and gummed paper cutouts. Pipe cleaner or construction paper arms and legs may be added as well. If a variety of found materials are made available, children will think of imaginative ways to transform tubes into people and animals.

Paper plate characters. The convex or outer side of a paper plate provides a perfect area for a puppet head. Children can choose from different found materials, as in tube puppets, to give their plates character. Parts of other plates can be cut up and attached for ears, noses, and handles. If the paper plate puppet is not to have a body, a tongue depressor or other stick may be attached for a handle.

Two other methods for creating sturdy handles by which children can manipulate the plates are plate pockets (Figure 12) and rolled newspaper rods (Figure 13). To make a pocket, another plate of the same size is cut in half and stapled to the upper portion of the back of the base plate before the puppet is begun.

To make a paper rod, roll a double or triple sheet of newspaper on the diagonal (very tightly) and tape the loose end down. Stapling the rod to the back of the plate puppet at top and bottom will keep it from becoming wobbly.

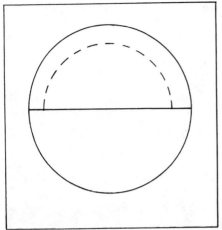

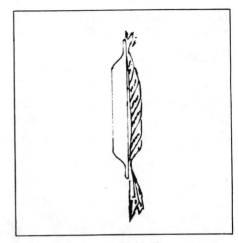

Fig. 12. Paper plate puppet.   *Fig. 13. Newspaper rod holder for puppet.*

The rod can be used for a plate puppet which is given a paper bag costume as well. After the bag is decorated, a small opening is cut in the closed end to allow the rod to pass through. The child inserts a hand into the open end of the bag, holding the puppet by the rod. If desired, floppy paper arms and legs may be attached to the paper bag to make the puppet more lifelike.

Finger puppets. Children can model simple puppet heads by placing small balls of self-hardening clay or dough clay on their fingers and pinching out the features. Children can paint the heads when dry and glue on hair, eyeballs, hats, and other items. Provide an assortment of fabric scraps for costumes. To dress this type of finger puppet, drape the fabric over the finger, and push the finger up into the little head.

Other finger puppets may be made of paper cutouts, rubber or Styrofoam balls, small boxes, glove fingers, and small plastic jars. If the finger cannot be placed into the object, a small ring can be made with a wire twist tie or a paper strip taped to the puppet.

Found objects puppets. Nonrepresentational puppet characters can be made by assembling various found materials. The main decisions will be which items to use for head and body parts and how to hold the puppets. Objects such as old socks, paper bags, and mittens are easy for children to manipulate and can be decorated with glued or sewed-on accessories. Imaginary creatures may be assembled by attaching paper boxes, scraps of Styrofoam, corks, pipe cleaners, plastic silverware, beads, and jar lids to each other.

There may be times when children want to sew costumes for their puppets. If children are familiar with interlacing (p. 95), it will not be difficult for them to devise simple stitched fabric tubes which can be attached to a neck tube with a rubber band. Cut finger holes as in Figure 14.

Scenery and stages. Children over six years of age who want to give a puppet show may decide to have scenery. Painted mural paper is an ideal backdrop for a doorway stage. The children sit on chairs or kneel and bring the puppets up from behind the paper, which has been taped to the door frame. If horizontal and vertical slits are cut in the mural scenery, children can insert stick puppets through them so that the characters appear to be moving on the painting as they are manipulated from behind.

A similar backdrop for a doorway stage can be created with strips of overlapping colored paper fastened tightly at the door frame sides. Strips can represent sky, roads, water, and so forth. Stick puppets can be pushed up and manipulated between these strips. Sabrina and Felicia, two first-grade girls, effectively created a water scene for their whale puppets by cutting out two strips of ocean waves to fasten in the doorway of their classroom.

A cardboard carton makes a fine puppet stage for stick puppets. The top is cut open to allow the puppets to be manipulated from above. The front is open and the box flaps are bent out to hold clipped-on, interchangeable drawings of the settings (Figure 15).

If children desire anonymity when they manipulate puppets, try a bridge table turned on its side, or a large carton from a refrigerator or a television. Cut away the back of the carton and cut off the top, adjusting the height to fit the children.

Fig. 14. Finger hole puppets.

Masks

Masks, like puppets, allow children to assume the character of others during their play. Such disguises may cover the child, her or his head, or the face alone.

Face masks. Children can decorate paper plates to use as masks in almost the same way they make plate puppets. The difference is that they must cut out eyes and mouths for seeing and speaking. Oval or round mask forms may also be made by laminating paper, following the process for instant papier-mâché (p. 83). Again, openings for seeing and speaking need to be cut. If a small wedge is cut from the laminated paper while it is still wet, this opening may be taped or stapled closed to give the mask more depth. Another type of face mask can be made with papier-mâché over a pie pan (p. 83).

Face masks may be decorated with tempera paint. Paper cutouts, yarn, feathers, cotton, and other lightweight material can also be attached. The masks are held on the head with string or with loops to place over the ears made of pipe cleaners or stapled-on rubber bands. These loops make it much easier for the child to put on and take off the mask.

Covered-head masks. Grocery bags are excellent bases for simple over-the-head masks. If the bags are large enough and extend to the knees, armholes may be cut and children can use them as one-piece masks/costumes. The paper bags can be painted and decorated in the same way as face masks.

To determine where to cut out the holes, the children should push the bags down on their heads, feel for their eyes and mouth on the outside, and carefully make a crayon mark at each prospective hole.

Large sheets of construction paper can also be made into attractive over-the-head masks. Form the paper into cones by stapling or taping the back together. The children paste on colored paper eyelashes, tongues, noses, antennae, ears, and horns. Paint can also be added for greater detail.

Open-face masks/costumes. Child-size characters can be drawn or painted on poster board and the face part cut out so that the children can place their own faces in it. If other poster boards are taped to the top backs of the first boards, children can wear the masks/costumes in sandwich-board fashion, suspending the sandwich boards from their heads. Children over five years of age may want to draw or paint the back of the character on the second board.

If you can obtain lightweight, washable foam core board, try cutting out several paddle-shaped face masks with eye holes (Figure 16). Children draw in hair, hats, ears, and facial features with chalk. These paddles can be wiped clean and used again many times.

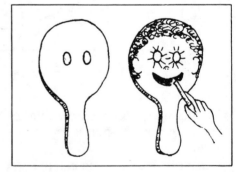

Fig. 15. Box for puppet stage.   *Fig. 16. Styrofoam masks.*

During their experiments with forming materials, children may try to attach parts of their artwork to each other or decorate items with fibers. Thus children come to understand something about interlacing as an art process.

Interlacing

It takes little effort to stimulate children's interest in stitchery, weaving, and knotting. Functional and decorative objects are daily reminders to children of these processes. When discussing types of interlacing with children, point out woven fabrics and grasses, knotted yarns, cord, stitched clothing, embroidered sofa pillows, and wall hangings in the environment.

Teachers and children can share their own rich cultural heritages by arranging handwork displays. Seeing and handling baskets, blankets, beadwork, and fancy stitchery made by people of different cultures can help children understand the potential of interlacing.

Stitchery

Children like to sew because they enjoy manipulating fibers in and out of different materials. Once the simple running stitch or overcasting stitch is mastered, children frequently use their new skill for attaching pieces of paper or fabric to one another. Children also discover that they can draw and decorate with stitches.

Punch and sew

Sewing on cards has always been one of the favorite manipulative experiences of young children. You can make cards for two- and three-year-old children, but most children over four years of age are able to punch their own holes around the perimeters of cut-out cardboard or plastic shapes. Children can also punch holes in the lines of drawings they made on pressed cardboard or Styrofoam supermarket trays. For very young children, provide strips of cardboard with one row of punched holes running down the length of the cardboard.

Two- and three-year-old children can use stiff-tipped shoelaces for sewing. If heavy yarn (four-ply worsted) is provided for sewing, knot one end and stiffen the sewing end by dipping it in glue and allowing it to harden, or wrap the tip with masking or cellophane tape.

Children over four years of age are usually able to handle blunt-end tapestry needles threaded with yarn. Keep a supply of threaded needles available for children to use. If you push a threaded needle through the short tail one or two times, you can secure it so that it does not come off during the sewing process (Figure 17).

Mesh stitchery

Before being given tightly woven fabrics for sewing, children can experiment with open weaves like inexpensive dixie mesh. In the beginning, children may seemingly haphazardly run yarn in and out of the little holes. After awhile, children ages five and older are able to draw a picture or form on the mesh and follow the drawn line with the needle and yarn as they did on sewing cards. Masking tape along the edges of the mesh will prevent fraying. Be sure to anchor the child's yarn with a knot to avoid the frustration of pulling out stitches.

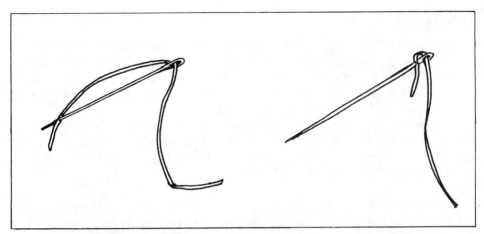

Fig. 17. Threaded needle.

Fabric stitchery

Children find that sewing with open-weave burlap or nylon net and a dull-pointed tapestry needle is easier than sewing with tightly woven fabrics like felt, muslin, and percale. As children become more experienced, make these fabrics and sharper needles available.

When children begin to sew, be sure the yarn is knotted at one end. You may have to demonstrate how the needle must move up and down through the fabric. If you are assisting a child who is left handed, remember to sew from left to right. Some children will find it easy to do a whip or overcasting stitch (Figure 18) along the edges of the fabric to join two pieces. Other children find that they have less trouble with a running stitch. Do not be discouraged if children in their early attempts at stitchery cross stitches or make a few tangles. Children are, after all, experimenting, as they do with other materials.

Once a few simple stitches for following a drawn design are mastered, six- to eight-year-old children are able to design and sew appliquéd forms to burlap or other fabric. The appliqués are best cut from felt because the edges of felt do not fray and therefore do not have to be turned under. To help beginners with appliqué, the cut felt shapes can be glued in place and then a few stitches made to tack them down. Thin yarn or embroidery floss is appropriate for this process. Many other helpful suggestions for stitching, stuffing, and embroidery are given in the two books by Fressard (1971) and Kornerrup (1967).

Weaving

The process of interlacing natural fibers to produce fabrics for clothing or floor and wall coverings comes to us from ancient civilizations. Weaving involves the interlacing of weaving fibers (the weft) over and under the stationary fibers (the warp). The closer the warp and weft threads are to each other, the tighter the weave. Coarse, heavy fibers produce thick, coarse fabric. Fine threads produce lightweight fabric.

Fibers children can use

Many fibers are suitable for beginning weaving. Heavy yarns, ribbons, cord, strips of fabric, string, plastic lacings, and straws produce interesting weavings. Natural materials such as feathers, grasses, and twigs can be included for accents. Children may also weave with flat or twisted paper.

To prepare twisted crepe paper quickly, cut a two-inch wide strip across the folded package of crepe paper and then unfold the strip. Attach one end of the paper to one beater of an electric hand mixer and the other end of the strip to a stationary object. Turn on the mixer to twist the strip. Stretched-out crepe paper streamers also make good paper fiber for weaving.

Children becoming more adept at weaving can string beads or tie pieces of contrasting yarn and feathers onto weaving threads. Children can also work on weaving techniques without a loom. Children may want to attach small pieces

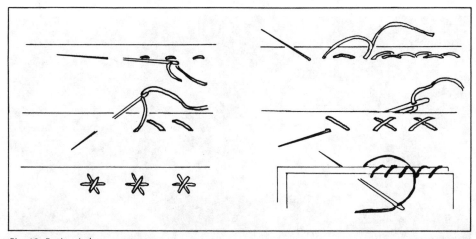

Fig. 18. Basic stitches.

of woven work to other art as decoration or as clothing for puppets. Six- to eight-year-old children might want to try related processes such as twisted yarn god's eyes or spool-knitted ropes.

Introducing weaving

One way to introduce children to weaving is to allow them to weave strips of cord or crepe paper in and out of the iron posts or wire mesh of a fence. If no fence is close by, try making a standing loom from a discarded oversize picture frame or an appliance carton with one side cut out. These large looms may be warped with heavy cord, and then children can weave in interesting fibers. After children have engaged in this type of cooperative weaving, provide smaller, individual looms.

Simple looms. Looms may be made from many materials, including cardboard, plastic coffee can lids, wire coat hangers, paper plates, shoe boxes, cigar boxes, dowel sticks, or twigs. The important first step is to attach warp threads. Cut an equal number of small slits on opposite sides to anchor the warp into the slits, and tie them in back. If you make a round loom, only an odd number of warp threads will work.

Paper looms. Children can try beginning weaving on a construction paper loom, too. To prepare the construction paper, cut five slits about 1½ inches apart down the length of a 9 × 12 inch sheet of construction paper. The slits can be made easily by folding the sheet of construction paper in half and cutting from the fold to within one and one-half inches from the edge. To make the mat weavings more decorative, try cutting zigzag or scalloped slits.

Provide the children with paper weaving strips cut from a variety of colored paper. The strips can be woven in and out of the cut-paper loom and the loose ends taped down in the back. To fill in the warp areas of this size paper loom, children will need six 1½ × 12 inch strips. Once woven and secured in place,

The process of interlacing natural fibers to produce fabrics for clothing or floor and wall coverings comes to us from ancient civilizations.

the strips can be personalized with crayon designs. Covering the finished weaving with adhesive-backed clear plastic will preserve it as a place mat.

A ladder loom which uses large strips of newspaper as both warp and weft is appropriate for most four- and five-year-old children to handle (Figure 19). For

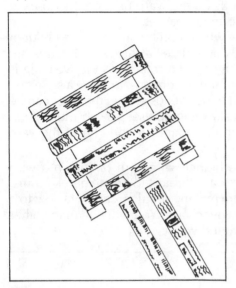

Fig. 19. Ladder loom.   Fig. 20. Circular loom.

the warp (ladder rungs) use sheets of newsprint or newspaper, folded lengthwise into two-inch-wide strips. Make seven such strips. Staple them to two side pieces of heavy cardboard strips to make the loom, allowing two inches between the paper strips. Four or five additional strips of folded paper of similar thickness are used as weaving strips (weft). When the weaving is complete, remove the cardboard, and tape under the loose ends. The woven newspaper is a perfect "sit-upon" mat for young children. It can be made more durable with a coat of shellac or spray enamel. Adhesive-backed plastic such as Contact paper, although expensive, is the best covering.

Circular loom. To make a loom from a paper plate, a cardboard circle, or a plastic coffee can lid, cut an odd number of slits around its edge. Wind the yarn or cord which will be the warp in crisscross fashion around the front and back of the plate, anchoring the warp in the slits. When you have used the last slit, fasten the short end of the yarn at the center back (Figure 20).

Using a tapestry needle, start the weaving at the center of the circular loom. Seven- and eight-year-old children who have worked on rectangular looms will be challenged to try this process. Remove the completed weaving from the loom by cutting through the yarn at the back center. The ends can be trimmed and knotted to hold the woven strands in place. A drop of white glue may be placed at the end of each spoke as well.

A cardboard circle or plate can also be used as a loom without need for a fiber warp. With this loom, the circle is cut into an odd number of radiating spokes (which act as the warp). As noted in Figure 21, spaces must be left in between the spokes to allow room for the fiber weft. This type of weaving can be used to form a basket. If the child pulls on the warp fiber gently on each round, it will pull up the cardboard to form the basket.

Box looms. This popular loom can be worked on by one or more children taking turns and weaving a few strands at a time. If the warp threads are wrapped completely around the box, they can be rotated as the weaving is completed on one portion to fashion belts and headbands. Prepare a shoe box loom for warping by cutting slits on both narrow ends so that the fiber can be anchored. A bobby pin or an ice cream stick can be used as substitutes for a needle. Carefully drill a small hole in the stick and tie the end of the yarn through it.

Quick looms. Wrap a Y-shaped tree branch with yarn or stretch a wire hanger into a diamond shape and tie on warp threads to create quick looms. Punched plastic, the cast-off material from making sequins, can be tacked to a frame and act as a warp which receives woven yarn. You will find many other possibilities if you are alert to objects around you.

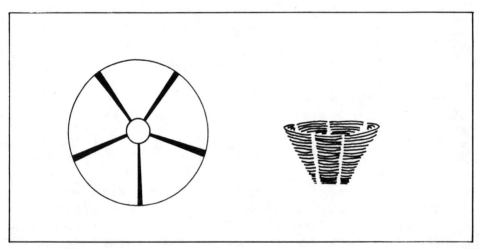

Fig. 21. Basket loom.

Knotting and looping

Children who are able to tie their shoes are usually able to knot and loop to make useful and decorative items. One skillful group of kindergarten children assembled several strands of colored yarn. Then the children made a series of overhand knots along the strands and ended up with handsome belts.

Six- to eight-year-old children can create a yarn chain by looping the fiber over a finger instead of a crochet hook (Figure 22). Tie one end of a ball of yarn into a loop. Place the loop on the index finger. Wind more of the yarn over the finger closer to the nail; pass the original loop over the wound strand and off the finger. Repeat this technique, pulling down on the tail of the yarn each time and you will have a chain which may be applied on other materials for decoration, or may be used as a necklace.

Five- and six-year-old children can tie a few lengths of colored yarn or cord to a dowel stick or twig to create a wall hanging. The strands can be attached to each other with half hitch knots and/or square knots. These techniques are described in detail in macramé instruction books.

Children over six years of age enjoy knotting cut pile on rug canvas. They draw their designs directly on the rug canvas with felt markers and then fill in the different areas with precut rug yarn. The knotting is done quickly with simple-to-operate latch hooks. Small mats and pillows made this way make attractive and practical gifts.

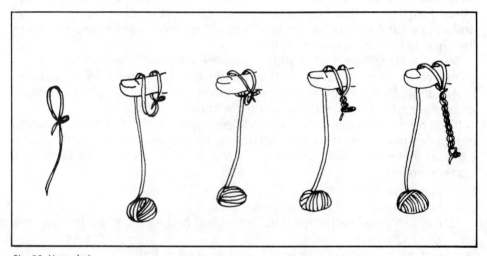

Fig. 22. Yarn chain.

Photographic techniques

Photography-related activities can make important contributions to early art education. Some processes sensitize children to the visual elements in the environment, while other processes bring together several of the applying techniques already discussed. Although most of the suggestions we include are appropriate for children over six years of age, some four- and five-year-old children may also be able to participate.

Building visual awareness

Making viewfinders

Small picture frame viewfinders help children zero in on the sights around them. Children can look out of the window through a viewfinder and observe parts of skylines, fields, or forests. Children who take viewfinders along on neighborhood walks or trips usually remember more details of what they have seen.

Follow these steps to make a viewfinder:

1. Fold a 5 × 7 inch sheet of drawing paper in half.
2. Begin at the fold, and cut or tear out a small rectangular shape. If the children are able to cut through two thicknesses of drawing paper at once, paste two sheets together to make a sturdier viewfinder. Older children may be able to cut oak tag or cardboard for this purpose.
3. Open the folded paper to reveal the viewing hole.

Using a camera

Taking pictures is a natural outgrowth of looking at things through a view-finder. Young children can learn how to operate a simple Instamatic-type camera. One group of kindergarten children produced a set of slides entitled Me and My House. The class took several walks in the school neighborhood and stopped at the home of each child so a classmate could snap a picture of the child in front of her or his home.

Seven- and eight-year-old children who are also able to work a fixed-focus 35 mm camera enjoy creating their own slide stories. Photography books listed in Appendix E present other interesting ways children of this age can photo-graph their artwork to create both still and movie productions.

If you have access to a darkroom and developing materials, you may want to introduce children over six years of age to the process for making their own cameras and prints. The pinhole camera is a simple example of the way a camera works:

Making a pinhole camera

1. Find a small cardboard box with a lid.
2. Pierce a one-fourth-inch hole in one end of the box with sharp scissors and twist them.
3. Cut out a one-inch square of heavy aluminum foil.
4. Pierce a hole in the center of the foil with a fine sewing needle.
5. Center and tape the foil over the one-fourth-inch hole in the box.
6. Tape all box joints except the lid with black tape, placing a bit of tape over the pinhole on the foil.
7. Take the box into a darkroom and tape a piece of fast film (Tri-X) to the side of the box opposite the pinhole. While in the darkroom, cover the box and tape closed all lid seams.
8. Take the camera outdoors and face it toward a well-lit object or scene. Set the camera down, remove the tape from the pinhole, and allow the light to enter this tiny hole for about 15 seconds.
9. Tape up the pinhole once again and take the camera into a darkroom to develop and print the film.

Making prints without a camera

Many of us have found, upon removing displays from bulletin boards, that the background paper has faded, leaving silhouettes of the mounted material in the original shade of the paper. Others of us remember how as children we pressed negatives of snapshots against "magic" paper and held them out in the sunshine to be printed. Young children can make creative arrangements of flat objects which they print by placing them on special papers and exposing them to the sun in this way, too. Construction paper and blueprint paper do not require dangerous chemical fixers.

Construction paper prints. Provide the children with sheets of red or blue construction paper which fit into cafeteria trays. The children arrange cut-out paper shapes; flat objects such as combs, scissors, jar lids, mesh, pieces of plastic tomato cartons, etc., into groupings on the colored paper. Lightweight items such as leaves, grasses, and paper cutouts print best if they are temporarily secured to the construction paper first with small amounts of white glue. Once the items are attached, tape the construction paper to a windowpane on the sunny side of the room, with the glued-on items facing the sun. If the sun is hazy, leave the paper on the window for several days. In bright sun, windowpane prints emerge in one or two days. If you take them out into the play yard in bright sunlight, the paper may fade in 15 minutes. To speed the sun's action, try coating the papers with carrot or red cabbage juice.

Blueprints. Photograms, another name for prints made without cameras, can be made quite inexpensively on blueprint paper. A 36-inch roll of this paper can be purchased from duplicating firms or architects. The only other needed item, three percent peroxide, is a safe liquid available in drugstores.

Follow these steps to make a blueprint:
1. Combine one gallon of water with one cup of peroxide in a pan or pail.
2. Prepare a pan of clear water for rinsing prints.
3. Cut off only the amount of blueprint paper to be used immediately (keep the rest well covered to extend shelf life).
4. Place the paper blue side up on a tray away from direct light.
5. Arrange a variety of two-dimensional objects on the paper as for construction paper sun prints. This process works best if the objects are flat against the paper. Thus, metal items such as scissors, keys, and jar lids are appropriate. Placing a sheet of glass over the arrangement of flat objects also assures a clearer print.
6. Place the arrangement in strong sunlight for one or two minutes (longer if the sun is hazy).
7. Remove the objects and immerse the blueprint paper in the peroxide solution until the background areas are bright blue and the object images show up white.
8. Rinse the paper in clear water and blot with paper towels.

Printing-out paper. This photographic paper, usually used for printing proofs, may be used the same way as blueprint paper. However, it is more expensive and requires a chemical fixer to make images permanent. Different companies manufacture this paper under a variety of names. Check with your local photography supply store to determine the most economical combination. We recommend that this process be used only with children who can handle the chemical fixer safely.

Drawing on film

Although young children ordinarily draw large images, some children ages five and older can draw small enough to create their own slides, filmstrips, transparencies, and 8 mm or 16 mm movies. Thirty-five mm camera film has the largest drawing area. Although discarded developed film this size may be bleached out with household bleach and used for drawing, it is advisable to purchase blank 35 mm film prepared with a special coating and sold under the name U Film. The film takes ordinary inks and markers, as well as colored pencils. Children who draw on this film can make individual slides and place them in 2 × 2 inch slide mounts. Seven- and eight-year-old children may want to create a picture story. The story can be planned on a paper storyboard (a series of rectangles drawn the same size as each film frame). The children draw their designs on the paper in the proper sequence and then trace them on the film.

Acetate sheets may be purchased, along with special audiovisual marker pens, from audiovisual supply firms. This transparent film, which teachers often use for instructional purposes, is also an excellent surface for child-made art transparencies. A source for free acetate is bleached out X-ray film. Ask your doctor or dentist to save discards. Young children can draw on the acetate, paste bits of colored tissue and cellophane on it, and project the images with an overhead projector for their own light shows. Small pieces of acetate can also be prepared as slides. Children arrange the tissue and/or cellophane between two 2 × 2 squares with the viewing area cut away, and tape the edges with masking tape. Commercial slide mounts may also be used for more durability, and plastic mounts may be used repeatedly.

Children ages six and older have fun drawing or scratching scribble designs on clear movie film leader with felt-tipped marking pens or special noncrawl inks. Suppliers also sell black leader on which scratches may be made with a sharp object. Exposed movie film may receive scratch designs, or clear it with household bleach to use for drawing. It is important to realize in drawing on movie film that it takes several frames (24 in 16 mm film) to recognize a projected image. Therefore, in a cooperative venture allow each child at least one foot of film. A workable procedure is to tape the film along the length and width of tables, give each child an assigned spot, and roll up the film as the drawings are completed, adding new blank footage. When several yards of film have been completed (drawn or scratched), thread the film into a projector for showing. Try playing some fast-tempo recorded music along with the film to delight the children.

Whether art materials are interlaced, formed, or applied, the personal expressiveness children exhibit when they engage in these processes depends largely on the quality of adult support and guidance.

We invite you to choose selectively from among the broad variety of processes and possibilities described in this chapter. Because there are many alternatives, two questions may assist you in your selections:

(1) What is the process's potential for stimulating the child's enthusiastic participation?

(2) To what degree does the process match the child's developmental needs?

This review chart should help you decide which processes are most appropriate for your children.

Art processes

Simple	More Complex
Tempera painting	Painting with watercolors
Finger painting	Printing from blocks
Making monoprints	Printing with stencils
Printing with found materials	Tie and dye
Roller painting (color mixing)	Batik
Dip and dye	Dropper blends and dribble trails
Drawing with crayons	Drawing with Payons
Making crayon rubbings	Charcoal sketching
Drawing with felt markers	Crayon sgraffito
Drawing with chalk	Drawing with Craypas
Drawing in sand	Making rub-off stencils
Paper tearing and cutting	Crayon resist
Paper collage, fabric collage	Drawing with pencils (see caution)
Preparing viewfinders	Drawing with glue
Taking Instamatic photos	Yarn painting
Making sun prints	Montage
Drawing on acetate	Mosaics
Clay modeling	Making slides, filmstrips, movies
Dough modeling	Making pinhole cameras
Wadded paper construction	Paper pulp modeling
Paper tube construction	Modeling with sawdust
Quick method papier-mâché	Clay/pottery techniques
Found materials assemblage	Sand casting
Wood scrap assemblage	Casting/carving plaster
Box construction	Paper sculpture
Woodworking	Cardboard construction
Plaster drop forms	Papier-mâché
Plaster waste molds	Mobiles
Stick puppets	Pariscraft puppet heads
Tube puppets	Sewn puppet clothes
Found object puppets	Open-face masks/costumes
Finger puppets	Fabric stitchery
Plate masks	Weaving on round looms
Bag masks	Weaving on box looms
Papier-mâché masks	Off-loom weaving
Mesh stitchery	Simple macramé
Weaving with paper	Knotting on rug canvas
Weaving on cardboard looms	Finger-chain looping
Weaving newspaper on ladder looms	
Weaving on quick looms	
Overhand knotting	

References

Fiarotta, P., and Fiarotta, N. *The You and Me Heritage Tree.* New York: Workman Publishing Co., 1976.

Fressard, M. J. *Creating with Burlap.* New York: Sterling Publishing, 1971.

Herberholz, B. *Early Childhood Art.* 2nd ed. Dubuque, Iowa: William C. Brown, 1979.

Hill, D. *Mud, Sand, and Water.* Washington, D.C.: National Association for the Education of Young Children, 1977.

Kornerrup, A-M. *Embroidery for Children.* New York: Van Nostrand Reinhold, 1967.

Wankelman, W.; Wigg, P.; and Wigg, M. *A Handbook of Arts and Crafts.* Dubuque, Iowa: William C. Brown, 1978.

Wiseman, A. *Making Things.* Boston: Little, Brown, *Book I,* 1967; *Book II,* 1975.

5
Creative Art Enhances Learning

Throughout this book we have noted the significance of creative art for young children's learning. This chapter will further examine those aspects of art activity which can enhance learning.

What do children learn through art?

Those who have some responsibility for nurturing growth and development in young children, whether they be parents, teachers, or other caregivers, are interested in knowing in some detail what children learn through creative art. Researchers have analyzed children's learning in terms of its physical/perceptual, cognitive, and social/emotional facets (Table 2) (Kellogg 1969; Piaget 1972; Mussen 1973; Larsen 1975; Bloom 1976; McCarthy 1980). However, especially with young children, learning is a complex process in which all aspects are intertwined and mostly occur simultaneously.

Three-year-old Mei Ling had already developed a distinct, colorful schema for representing her favorite art subject—flowers. In addition, her flower paintings included controlled strokes resembling Chinese calligraphy. When the teacher asked if she could keep the flower picture until the next day, Mei Ling said softly, "Me take home." The teacher explained that she wanted to show it to the teachers who would be coming that night. The teacher tried further coaxing and reassuring. However, Mei Ling quietly and affirmatively concluded, "Me take home."

At age three, Mei Ling represented her perceptual and aesthetic awareness of flowers in a variety of shapes and colors. She exhibited unusual dexterity in her Chinese writing, which she understood to be a part of her culture. She also asserted herself skillfully to claim her valued work. Although we will now look at three areas of learning through art, the reader must keep in mind how all are integrated in the child's development.

Physical/perceptual development

Exploring and creating with art materials helps children become more sensitive to the physical environment (Franck 1973; McFee 1977; Kauppinen

1980). Powers of perception improve as children visually and kinesthetically sense impressions of color, line, form, and texture. The ability to discriminate among these elements of design begins as experimentation with materials continues. Color, line, form, and texture become part of children's visual vocabulary.

Table 2. Children Learn Through Art

Physical/perceptual development	Cognitive development	Social/emotional development
Tactile-kinesthetic awareness	Clarify and elaborate meaning	Sense of trust
Visual awareness	Associate related information	Sense of identity/individuality
Spatial awareness	and ideas	Sense of
Body awareness	Sequence events	autonomy/independence
Eye-hand coordination	Understand cause and effect	Express and deal positively with
Laterality and directionality	Solve problems	emotions
Shape, size, color discrimination	Make decisions	Extend flexibility
Figure-ground orientation	Generalize	Aesthetic growth
Part-whole discrimination	Communicate ideas	Appreciate and value others'
Fine motor control	nonverbally	ideas and work
Technical skills		Share
		Cooperate
		Take turns (delay gratification)
		Adapt to group needs/interests
		Resolve interpersonal conflicts
		Acquire interests for leisure time

When children start to perceive differences in color, they experiment with light and dark hues and tints and mixtures. Contrasts of brilliants and dulls and warms and cools are juxtaposed for effect. Linear patterns are created with two- and three-dimensional art media. Children can make sharp lines, curved lines, coils, and squiggles with paint, crayon, string, yarn, and wire. In rural areas children observe the slant of tall wheat and grasses, while urban children notice the sharp contrasts in city skylines. The variety of lines in these environments can be represented by printing with the edge of a piece of cardboard or the side of a tongue depressor.

Increased ability to discriminate among textures develops through creative art. Children use a variety of papers and fabrics for collages, rub crayons over different materials, and print with many objects on diverse surfaces. Opportunities to learn about texture abound at the workbench: the roughness of sandpaper, the smoothness of the dowel stick, and the sharpness of the wood splinter. Textured art materials help children reinforce knowledge about the physical appearance of people and animals. Yarn, cotton, and fur fabric may be used for people's hair, beards and mustaches, and animal coats.

Explorations with art materials offer opportunities to sharpen perceptions of form. Children note relationships between artistic two- and three-dimensional forms and the environment: "My clay is round like a pizza pie," "I drew a square like the book," or "Look at the funny shape of my puppet's head; it's not like my head." These expressions indicate that children are learning about form while engaging in the creative process. Visual acuity is implicit in all art activity and is an attribute that needs to be developed for beginning reading.

The use of found materials to create art demonstrates that children's thinking about form is being enhanced. For example, a child may add a paper cup to a clay ball to form an ice cream cone or fold a paper plate over a clay hamburger to make a roll.

Children also develop manual dexterity and fine motor coordination during the creative art process. Cutting, sewing, drawing, hammering, and painting help children refine eye-hand coordination skills which are necessary for manipulating the things they use daily, as well as for writing. Such skills appear to be more pleasurably developed through art than through repetitive and unimaginative completion of duplicated work sheets.

A growing perception of figure-ground orientation occurs when three- and four-year-old children begin to make and name enclosed shapes. Children gradually move beyond the head-feet symbol for people to include more detail and accurate placement of human anatomy. The expressed relationship of parts to the whole shows greater perceptual awareness.

Increased perceptual awareness is revealed in many other ways in children's art. Art expression helps to stabilize perceptual learning so that children can use their awareness with greater consistency. Cognitive growth is supported as perceptual knowledge and physical growth become assimilated into thought processes.

Children also develop manual dexterity and fine motor coordination during the creative art process.

Cognitive development

In the process of creating visual images, young children use art to communicate information and feelings. As children grow and develop, visual images of experiences are personal symbols rather than camera-like reproductions. Subjective art impressions may convey information which children may not be ready or able to express through words. The visual image helps children clarify or reinforce the ideas.

One day three-year-old Felicia was busy making crayon symbols on her paper. She chanted over and over again as she worked, "My Mommy went to Washington."

Children learn more about themselves and their capabilities through art.

Hearing the chant, her teacher suggested, "I guess she went on business."

"No, of course not," retorted Felicia. "She went on a jet plane as big as this," she added, as she swept her crayon across her paper and onto the table.

"Yes," affirmed the teacher, "she traveled on a very big jet plane in order to do her business work in Washington."

"That's what I said," replied the articulate three-year-old child.

Art activity with a variety of materials enhances thinking skills. The characteristics of different items are compared and relationships discovered between the new and the already familiar. Children associate particular tools with certain processes and learn which tools work best with various materials. For example, a thin brush will make a thin line with paint, and a thick one creates a broader stroke. A sharp needle is needed to sew through felt, but a blunt end works well for open-weave fabrics.

Although young children do not yet have stable concepts of time, they do deal with some aspects of time. They frequently seem verbally to practice a sequence of events: after we eat, we listen to records; we put on our boots; then we go home. Children's monologues while painting or drawing may reveal sequences of events important to them, although not recognizable to others from the children's private symbols. In a later stage, the correct or logical sequence of events is scrupulously observed in creating a series of illustrations for a movie made by joining pictures to tell a story. Thus, concepts of *before and after,* as well as *cause and effect,* which are expressed and clarified through art activities, are likely to be assimilated into a child's cognitive structure.

Chapter 3 contains many examples of how art activities foster problem solving, require choosing and decision making, and lead children to useful generalizations. Perhaps the relationship between art activities and cognitive growth has not been given the emphasis it deserves.

Brittain (1979) summarized considerable research on art and young children:

> There is something exciting for children in the organizing and abstracting process which is a necessary part of producing art. This is not a passive activity, but one which encompasses all of the senses, each providing some input into an operational system which creates new forms that are constantly altered through an interaction process. The activity of bringing together and elaborating upon the essence of the external world, coupled with the physical activity of exploring through the use of color, form, and space, provides an opportunity to develop a reality which in a broad sense could be considered knowledge. (p. 198)

Social/emotional development

Explorations with art materials are pleasurable activities for young children. Children who are still in the sensorimotor stage of development or have recently grown out of it are excited by the stimulation of varicolored paints, the contrasting qualities of soft clay and hard lumber, and the many types of wet and dry media. Very young children delight in covering sheets of newsprint with broad brush strokes of shiny wet tempera paint or prodding and pounding masses of clay and dough into peaks and valleys. Older children find satisfaction in building with wood or cooperating to complete a mural story.

In addition to the enjoyment arising from the use of art materials, children learn more about themselves and their capabilities and affirm their sense of self (Feldman 1970; Dimondstein 1974; Beittel 1979). A child at the easel has used many bright colors and is proud of his accomplishment. "I'm Herbie. I like to paint pretty colors. Write my name at the top," he calls out to a visitor. This three-year-old child's growing concept of self is evident as he views what he has painted.

The creative process offers opportunities for children to gain a spirit of independence and a sense of personal autonomy when the choice of medium, process, or kind of expression is their own (Lasky 1972; Cohen and Rudolph 1977). The good feelings about themselves which can be fostered through art are essential for developing personalities. Many possibilities for this development exist when children can record personal impressions visually. Their creations, eyes, and voices exclaim, "See me; see what I can do!"

Self-initiated successful endeavors in art can establish positive attitudes toward school. Normally shy six-year-old Kathy proudly displayed the tree ornament which she fashioned from two red cookie papers. "Look, I made a queen of the angels!" she exclaimed to her teacher. "Can I bring my mother to see it?" Before that day Kathy had been reluctant about coming to school. The completion and display of her art caused a marked change in her attitude about attending school.

Adults who observe young children using art materials for their own purposes are impressed by children's competence, sense of self, and independence. The children see in their artwork visible evidence of their competence and ability to influence the outside world. The climate for expressiveness (Chapter 3, p. 24) is important in helping children develop a sense of trust and autonomy and a growing awareness of individuality. All this and more is learned from art (Reichenberg-Hackett 1964; Dimondstein 1974; Herberholz 1979).

The creative art process allows children to visually translate personal feelings as well as ideas (Dewey 1958; Lowenfeld and Brittain 1975). Art thus becomes an emotional catharsis. The use of color and the size or placement of representations frequently reflect healthy emotions which are difficult to express in words. While it is important for teachers to be aware of this value of art for children, analysis of emotional problems should be referred to a professional psychologist if other behavior also indicates children may have difficulties.

It is not unusual for a teacher to notice that children vigorously pounding clay or energetically hammering nails seem to be relieving tension or frustration. Children who are afraid of the dark may have to paint some brown or black or purple renditions. Bright colors or symbols of smiling faces may express happy experiences. Art as a vent for feeling is universally acknowledged for artists of all ages (Lowenfeld and Brittain 1975; Lansing 1976).

A sense of aesthetics develops when art material is used creatively (Eisner 1972; Lansing 1976; Arts, Education and Awareness Panel 1977). The beauty of the world is translated into artwork. Some favorite themes of children are flowers, rainbows, fancy clothes, and accessories. Children's art will further enhance aesthetic learning if there are opportunities to create functional things of beauty for the classroom. For example, children can create wallpaper and curtains for the housekeeping area, make centerpieces and placemats for parties, and arrange bulletin boards to display artwork. This process of creation, which may include gifts for loved ones, builds a foundation for aesthetic appreciation which enriches life.

Careful work also becomes appreciated and valued. Children begin to understand the necessity for tools and how to care for them. Children become more flexible by learning that many projects can be accomplished in more than one way.

Many opportunities for social learning arise when children work near each other with art materials. Contributions of classmates are observed and valued and children learn to respect the needs and capacities of others to engage in

Many opportunities for social learning arise when children work near each other with art materials.

both independent thought and cooperative action. Such insight and understanding gained in the early years may lead children to more successful participation as adult members of our democratic society.

Because young children are naturally egocentric, they face the difficult, yet necessary, task of moderating their self-interest to cope with group living. Young children must learn the self-discipline inherent in cooperating, in delaying gratification, and in adapting when necessary to group interests and needs. Skill in resolving interpersonal conflicts gradually develops. Creative art activities that take place in an open and flexible atmosphere provide a valuable setting for these psychosocial learnings.

Children working with art materials make scientific observations.

Other important social learnings, which are also part of the social studies curriculum, will be discussed in some detail in the next section of this chapter.

How fortunate that art experiences which give children so much pleasure should also be so effective in helping them to learn about themselves, other people, and how better to negotiate the real conditions of group living. Art processes that children learn about and enjoy can continue to serve as sources of enrichment throughout life. Some children will go on to study art as a profession. Others will turn to art activities as a source of leisure-time enjoyment.

How is art related to other curriculum areas?*

Art activity has been a traditional component of early childhood programs, not only because it is personally rewarding for children and enhances their development, but because it provides a natural means for integrating learning from other curriculum areas. For example, we know that social studies topics may be introduced, clarified, or reinforced through art and that language arts can be enhanced when children engage in art explorations (Cohen and Gainer 1976; Seefeldt 1977).

Because our practice is based on sound principles of child development, we expect children to learn through art in their own ways and at their own pace. Although some three-year-old children may verbalize fluently about a topic, they may not yet be ready graphically to represent anything about that topic.

Subject-related learning through art for young children can be of two kinds:

(1) incidental learning as a by-product of children's use of particular media, materials, techniques, or processes, and

(2) guided learning as children engage in art activities planned by the teacher.

Incidental learning occurs, for example, when Justin discovers that his clay becomes too thin when he adds a lot of water and will no longer hold its shape (science); or when Brenda finds that she needs one more brush as she places a brush in each container of different-colored paint (mathematics). In contrast, guided learning may occur when the teacher encourages children to design tickets for use on the play train constructed in the block area (mathematics and social studies). Guided learning may also develop when the teacher plans activities related to a topic in which the children are interested.

When the four-year-old children were discussing the people in their families, Frederico exclaimed, "Today is my brother's birthday." The teacher encouraged Frederico and his friends to design birthday cakes with the appropriate number of candles on them (math and social studies).

Incidental learning through art

Science

Children working with art materials make scientific observations, noting that water makes tempera paint thinner and that crayons and Plasticine become soft if left near the heat. Chrissy looks at her drippy wet painting and exclaims, "I wonder if I can blow it dry with my wind." David finds that his clay banana left on the windowsill overnight has "gotten all hardened up" because it is no longer wet.

Experimentation with art materials may lead to many other discoveries about cause and effect. Children notice that colors change as they are mixed and that the sponges used for printing absorb liquid. In contrast, other materials such as plastics are found to be nonabsorbent. Children using many materials

---

*The authors are indebted to Betty Rowan of the University of Miami for some of the material included in this section.

observe differences between liquids and solids and see that other items such as wax crayons and oil paints resist water. In mixing paint from powder, children learn that some materials dissolve in water. The operations of simple machines can be understood through using tools such as scissors and hammers. The potential for developing science concepts is in the art materials and in the processes—ready to be discovered and applied.

Mathematics

Other incidental learnings which can be acquired during art activity relate to mathematics. When materials are used for a particular process, children need to remember quantities and their order of use. Children can frequently be heard explaining a process to classmates by saying, "First you tear the strips, then you add the wheat paste, next you stick them on the balloon." As art projects are planned, children need to consider the number of items needed and perhaps the shapes that will be required.

We hear, "My truck will have four wheels," and "I need a triangle shape of wood for the roof of my house." Children will need to decide how many as they draw and paint: how many eyes on the face, fingers on the hand, and buttons on the coat.

Differences and equivalences in number and size frequently concern children. Six-year-old Jonathan calls out, "I want 10 feathers on my peacock, and I only have 9." Brian, sitting next to him, responds, "I have more than you; I have 12 feathers."

Carol and Diane are sitting together as they draw with crayons. The teacher overhears their conversation. "My red crayon is longer than yours."

"Now I have two blacks because mine broke."

"Look how small my yellow is!"

Children also learn about one-to-one correspondences as materials are chosen and distributed to classmates. Four children need four scissors. Five paste cups need five lumps of paste. Three needles need three lengths of yarn.

Vocabulary

An expanding vocabulary about art materials and processes is a natural partner to the activity itself. Children working with art materials will use descriptive terms for the media and the resulting creations. The teacher's use of particular words to compare size, weight, color, texture, and shape influences children's descriptions of their artwork. Previous knowledge is combined with new information as oral language develops. "Gushy, mushy wet paint," chanted three-year-old Elizabeth as she pushed the finger paint around on the tabletop. "Gushy, mushy red paint," responded one of her tablemates.

As children grow and develop through art, they begin to use words such as thick, thin, hard, soft, straight, curved, dark, light, smooth, and sticky. Vocabulary that indicates direction is also quickly assimilated into children's arena of understanding when they work with art materials. Five-year-old children show

how much they have learned with statements like these: "I wrote my name at the top"; "I put a board under the clay"; and "I drew smoke coming out of the chimney." Four-year-old Ronni told her mother that her teacher had framed one of her paintings and "stapled it right in the middle of the bulletin board."

Communications

Children who have difficulty expressing themselves through oral language often can indicate conceptual development through visual expression (Hamlin, Mukerji, and Yonemura 1967; Cohen and Gainer 1976). Records of sequential drawings made by aphasic children over a period of time have shown increased conceptual development as well as improved ability to organize ideas. A kindergarten boy who hardly used any oral language clearly indicated his conceptual understanding by the great detail he included in his drawing of a rabbit (Silver 1966).

Reading

When teachers label artwork or art materials, children begin to associate the written symbol with spoken language, a necessary reading skill (Bookbinder 1975; Eisner 1977; Hall 1979; Jansson and Schillereff 1980). If the stories told about art are written next to their work, children begin to understand that thoughts can be expressed through written words as well as through oral and pictorial descriptions.

Many of the incidental learnings from creative art are integrated into children's repertoire of understandings so that these learnings can be transferred to other situations. One day Chin wanted to prop up a toy he had brought from home for display on the kindergarten "come and see" table. He found a piece of cardboard, bent it into an easel, and taped it to the back of his toy. From past experience in using cardboard for artwork, Chin knew that this stiff material could support his toy.

Art serves as a stimulus for incidental learning when children explore and discover with materials. However, it is the personal meaning derived from the experience that helps children to integrate new ideas into existing internal structures. When opportunities present themselves, guided art activities that teachers plan or spontaneously suggest can also provide the kinds of personal experiences that directly foster children's acquisition of subject-related knowledge.

Guided art activities

Early childhood programs are frequently organized around topics of interest to young children. Because media and materials provide stimulating sense experiences which are essential to early learning, many teachers plan for or suggest art experiences to children which can help them understand more about a topic (Arnheim 1969; Isaacs 1974; Randhawa and Coffman 1978; Madeja 1978; Linderman and Herberholz 1979; Silver 1978). During the ac-

tivities, teachers may comment and question or point out relationships between the artwork and the topic. Frequently conversations between children
will be stimulated by the art activity. As a result, children learn, clarify, and
extend concepts about the topic from each other as well.

Social studies

We can see from some of the preceding conversations that when children
use art materials together, many incidental social learnings can occur. Children may begin to realize social concepts: "I am an important person who can
do many things; other people have needs similar to mine; working together
saves time and effort; taking turns avoids confusion; it is fun to work and play
with friends; and other people have good ideas." Here are the beginnings of
feelings of self-worth, sharing, and understanding about the interdependence
of living things.

In addition to learning how to be a member of the classroom community,
children also encounter aspects of the social studies curriculum that relate to
how people work and meet their needs as members of the larger society
(Feldman 1970; Robison 1977; Spodek 1978). Children may begin to build a
concept of the public right to community facilities such as roads, bridges, and
tunnels.

One day Mario and Tony were playing with blocks in the kindergarten
classroom. They decided that they needed a tunnel for the toy train to pass
through. They noticed that Anne had taken some boxes to make an assemblage. Among them was an oatmeal carton.

Mario to Anne:	Could we have that round box?
Anne:	No, I need it. What do you want it for?
Tony:	We want to make a tunnel.
Anne:	I'll make it and I'll paint it green.
Mario:	OK. But hurry up!
Anne:	(ten minutes later): Here's the tunnel. Now I'll play with the train.
Tony:	You can play because the tunnel is for everyone. Right?

There is more than fairness and cooperation in the preceding example: there is
the hint of children forming a key social studies concept.

Three topics which are often included among those considered appropriate
for young children are self and family, animals and pets, and transportation.
Curriculum guides will often suggest particular concepts which can be developed through the study of these topics.

We have selected several possible concepts for children's learning for each
of these topics and have listed a variety of related art activities for young children which can make significant contributions to their thinking. Examples of
children learning through this planned method will be included to illustrate the
integrated manner in which art activity and conceptual development can take
place. See Chapter 4 for specific information about art processes.

If the stories told about art are written next to their work, children begin to understand that thoughts can be expressed through written words as well as through oral and pictorial descriptions.

Self and family. Suggested concepts:
- I am an important person.
- Other people are important, too.
- People are alike in some ways and different in others.
- I am part of a family or group.
- People in families and groups care for and help each other.
- Other families may have the same or different customs from mine.

Suggested art activities:
1. Offer finger paint or water-based ink for making handprints and footprints.
2. Provide plaster of paris for making molds of hands from Plasticine models.
3. Encourage children to cut or tear out and paste magazine pictures which show people or families of different ages or cultures having fun or working together.
4. Keep a supply of pictures of people available for very young children to paste into books. Older children might wish to mount the pictures as a mural on a background they have prepared with other media.
5. Provide a variety of media and found materials for the children to make puppets of themselves or their families.
6. Encourage older children to draw self-portraits and transfer them onto unbleached muslin to sew and stuff as dolls or pillows.
7. Trace the shape of children's bodies as they lie down on large sheets of paper. Children can dress these life-size figures with fabric, felt, yarn, buttons, and beads.
8. Keep available an array of found materials for making dress-up accessories such as jewelry, hats, or masks.
9. Encourage children who can draw, paint, or model themselves and their families in personally meaningful ways: Me and My Best Friend; I Am Playing with My Favorite Toy; I Am Helping at My House; My Family at Dinner Time; My Family Went to . . . ; My Wish. These renditions can be used for cooperative murals, booklets, and jigsaw puzzles.

As children engage in these or similar art activities, discussions about parts of the body, members of the family and roles, family customs, and similar topics can be initiated by the teacher. One day after identifying family members from photographs which kindergarten children brought to school, the following incident occurred at a table where a few children had gathered to use clay.

Teacher: Perhaps one of you would like to model the people in your family with clay.

Jennifer: Look, this ball could be me. (She showed a two-inch sphere she had been rolling, added a small lump for a nose, and pushed her index finger into the ball, holding it aloft.) Now it's a puppet of me.

Bruce: It has no eyes or mouth.

Scott: I can make a better puppet. I'll push buttons into the clay for eyes.

Bruce: I made a bigger ball, so I can be the father bear, and we'll have a puppet show of the three bears.

Jennifer: Good, I'll make some porridge. (She added some bits of clay and water to a bowl.) Scott, you can be the baby. Anyway, your puppet is the littlest.

Bruce: Hey, my mother says fathers can cook too, so I'll make the porridge.

A single suggestion from the teacher led the children to a discussion of concepts about family members, their roles, and their comparative sizes, even though it was carried on within the context of "The Three Bears." The children identified parts of the face symbolically and demonstrated a developing sense of self-identity. Later on, creative dramatics with the clay puppets further clarified and reinforced these concepts. At other times, the teacher initiated discussions about porridge, favorite foods, and who does the cooking in the home. Thus, the art activity integrated several concepts related to self and the family.

Animals and pets. Suggested concepts:
- Animals are living things.
- All animals require food and water to live.
- Birds, reptiles, mammals, fish, insects, and amphibians are animals.
- Animals can differ from each other in appearance, the way they move, what they eat, the sounds they make, and where they live.
- Tame animals kept by people are called pets.
- Some animals are raised on farms for work or food.
- A zoo is a place where wild animals are kept so that people can see them safely.

Suggested art activities:
1. Encourage older children to draw, paint, or model representations of their pets doing something characteristic.
2. Suggest to children that they find pictures for collages about animals which live in different places, move in various ways, or have different body coverings.
3. Provide opportunities for children to make their drawings, paintings, or paste-ups of animal cutouts into booklets, murals, jigsaw puzzles, or puppets.
4. Offer a variety of boxes, trays, and found objects which children can use to make zoo cages or farm environments for toy animals or models they create.

5. Provide scraps of furry fabrics, yarn, or spotted and striped papers in different shapes which children can use to paste on a background, and then add appendages for real or imaginary animals.
6. Make a variety of boxes, cardboard tubes, and other found objects available so children can create real or imaginary creatures.
7. Guide children to create environments for classroom pets with plastic bottles, wood, clay, and natural materials such as sand, pebbles, shells, and seedpods.
8. Provide Styrofoam trays on which children can draw simple animal forms. Pierce the outline at regular intervals for the younger children to stitch. Older children can stitch through the trays themselves.
9. Transfer children's animal drawings onto felt or burlap. Cut out two duplicate shapes, stitch together, and fill with beans, seeds, or shredded nylon hose for use as toys to toss.
10. Encourage children to create all-over textures with various media on plain paper. (Simulate hair, fur, or feathers with finger paint or crayon.) Then cut out animal shapes.

Young children by touching, seeing, hearing, or smelling animals will be stimulated to use art media for animal representations. Children with an emotional attachment to household or school pets will be additionally motivated to create visual images. Teachers create opportunities for guided learning about animals by providing art media and materials for children to use; engaging children in discussions about animals; and reading stories, showing pictures, and singing songs about animals.

When two- and three-year-old children find that collage materials include scraps of furry fabric, symbols of favorite animals can be made by gluing scraps to cardboard or construction paper. As the particular animals are named, the teacher knows the children have integrated the concept that some animals have fur as a body covering. The relationship drawn between the animal and the art materials indicates that learning has occurred.

Sometimes after a trip to a zoo or farm, children will be stimulated visually to express their ideas about animals. After the class trip to the zoo, four-year-old Chan painted an elephant immediately upon returning to school. "Look, elephants are so funny because they have a tail on both ends," he announced. The teacher accepted Chan's work but, realizing his confusion, clarified the differences between a trunk and a tail. This example shows how art can serve as a vehicle for direct learning by helping children express their understandings. At the same time, the art responses give the teacher clues for further planning.

Learning about animals and pets can also take place as a result of spontaneous discovery and subsequent engagement in teacher-guided art activity. One day while his kindergarten class was out playing, Joseph found a grasshopper in the field. "Can we keep him, Miss B?" he begged. By asking pointed questions and providing materials, the teacher guided the children's thinking about how best to keep the insect. She offered a clear plastic cup into which the children decided to put some moist earth and grass. Joseph decided to cover the cup with a piece of paper held on with a rubber band. "I'll make some holes for air to go in," he responded in answer to a question by the teacher.

Although the insect was set free after one day, several children spent a good deal of time observing it. The teacher suggested that the magnifying glass could be used and guided the children by asking questions: "How does the grasshopper see?" "How are its eyes different from ours?" "Which legs seem to help him jump?" "How are they different from others?" The detailed drawings of grasshoppers made the next day indicated that the questions had motivated keen observation. Joseph, whose personal attachment to the insect was the greatest, created five different representations of the insect.

Transportation. Suggested concepts:

- Transportation is the moving of things or people from place to place.
- Animals and machines help transport things and people.
- Some machines used for transportation are trains, buses, cars, airplanes, and boats.
- Some machines move on land; some in the air; some in water; and some in space.
- Machines usually need trained drivers to steer them.
- People who are driven in machines are called passengers.
- Transporting things and people costs money.

Suggested art activities:

1. Encourage older children to draw, paint, and model themselves riding in a favorite vehicle or on an animal of transport.
2. Stimulate six- to eight-year-old children to think imaginatively about vehicles of the future and then depict them visually.
3. Provide pages for books on which children can paste shapes of vehicles.
4. Give children an opportunity to draw or paint a sequence story about a trip on an accordion-folded strip of shelving paper. This can be done cooperatively or individually by children over six years of age. The same activity can be done using marking pens on a window shade still on a roller.
5. Provide an assortment of squares, rectangles, triangles, and circles which children can paste together in their own ways to create real or imaginary vehicles.
6. Make available an assortment of cardboard boxes, tubes, etc. which children can assemble into trains, cars, trucks, and planes.
7. Encourage the creation of vehicles using wheels made of sliced dowel

and broomsticks, as well as jar lids and empty spools.

8. Provide large cartons for children to paint and decorate for use as dramatic play vehicles.
9. Encourage children to cut out cardboard silhouettes of vehicles which can be used as stencils.
10. Provide an assortment of found materials which children can combine, assemble, or decorate for use as accessories in dramatic play about transportation (e.g., hats and helmets, binoculars, control panel, and tickets).
11. Give children an opportunity to paint mural backgrounds of water, land, and air environments for pasting on cutouts of vehicles children have drawn or painted.
12. Provide scraps of Styrofoam into which children can put sticks, sails, etc., for boats to float in small tubs.

The integration of concepts related to modes of travel is easily accomplished when children create their own props for dramatic play. Even without firsthand experiences, most children, while watching television, have vicariously ridden in different kinds of vehicles.

When the excitement from the moon exploration figured prominently in the news, the children in Mrs. W's first-grade class were stimulated by both the news and their teacher's plans with them to engage in many art activities. With the teacher's guidance, the children built a frame for a seven-foot high rocket and covered it with burlap. Then they painted the fabric with silver paint. They designed a control panel complete with knobs, numerals, and arrows. A battery-operated flashlight provided interior and signal light. Several children designed ground-to-crew control panels complete with pipe cleaner and cardboard headphones. Pieces of foil, rubber bands, paper fasteners, marking pens, and box lids were handy accessories for the children's creations. As the interest in space travel continued, the walls of the corridor outside of the classroom became covered with striking paintings of spaceships and would-be astronauts. Clay and papier-mâché constructions of moon craters were made to provide landing places for the small cardboard tube rocket ships some of the children devised. Experience charts were illustrated with drawings by the children, and the words *countdown, crater, gravity,* and *orbit* soon became part of the conversation. The teacher provided art materials, books, photographs, songs, and games, as well as time for discussion and for the children to create their artwork. Social studies, science, mathematics, and language arts experiences were abundant throughout these many activities. The opportunities to engage in creative art helped children to integrate many learnings and both clarified and reinforced their understandings.

Spontaneous and planned art experiences provide a wealth of possibilities for young children to assimilate knowledge about their world. Art not only connects with other curriculum areas; it connects with life.

Through the process of creating beautiful things, children begin to build a foundation for aesthetic appreciation which enriches life.

References

Arnheim, R. *Art and Visual Perception.* Berkeley, Calif.: University of California Press, 1969.

Arts, Education and Awareness Panel. *Coming to Our Senses: The Significance of the Arts for American Education.* New York: McGraw-Hill, 1977.

Beittel, K. R. "Teaching of Art in Relation to Body Mind Integration and Self Actualization in Art." *Art Education* 32 (Nov. 1979): 18-20.

Bloom, B. S. *Human Characteristics of School Learning.* New York: McGraw-Hill, 1976.

Bookbinder, J. "Art and Reading." *Language Arts* 52, no. 6 (1975): 783-785, 796.

Brittain, W. L. *Creativity, Art and the Young Child.* New York: Macmillan, 1979.

Cohen, D., and Rudolph, M. *Kindergarten and Early Schooling.* Englewood Cliffs, N.J.: Prentice-Hall, 1977.

Cohen, E. P., and Gainer, R. S. *Art: Another Language for Learning.* New York: Citation, 1976.

Dewey, J. *Art as Experience.* New York: Capricorn Books/G. P. Putnam's Sons, 1958.

Dimondstein, G. *Exploring the Arts with Children.* New York: Macmillan, 1974.

Eisner, E. W. *Educating Artistic Vision.* New York: Macmillan, 1972.

Eisner, E. W. "Reading, the Arts, and the Creation of Meaning." Reston, Va.: National Art Education Association, 1977.

Feldman, E. B. *Becoming Human Through Art.* Englewood Cliffs, N.J.: Prentice-Hall, 1970.

Franck, F. *The Zen of Seeing.* New York: Vintage, 1973.

Hall, B. A. "The Arts and Reading: Coming to Our Senses—Why the Visual and Performing Arts are Fundamental to Reading and Language Development." Paper presented at Annual Meeting of the Claremont California Reading Conference, Jan. 1979. ERIC ED 170 706.

Hamlin, R.; Mukerji, R.; and Yonemura, M. *Schools for Disadvantaged Young Children.* New York: Teachers College Press, Columbia University, 1967.

Herberholz, B. *Early Childhood Art.* 2nd ed. Dubuque, Iowa: William C. Brown, 1979.

Isaacs, N. *Children's Ways of Knowing.* New York: Teachers College Press, Columbia University, 1974.

Jansson, D. R., and Schillereff, T. A. "Reinforcing Remedial Readers Through Art Activities." *Reading Teacher* 33 (Feb. 1980): 548-551.

Kauppinen, H. "Environmental Awareness Through Art: The Finnish Approach." *School Arts* 79 (March 1980): 22-25.

Kellogg, R. *Analyzing Children's Art.* Palo Alto, Calif.: National Press Books, 1969.

Lansing, K. M. *Art, Artists, and Art Education.* Dubuque, Iowa: Kendall/Hunt, 1976.

Larsen, S. C., and Hammill, D. D. "The Relationship of Selected Visual Perceptual Abilities to School Learning." *Journal of Special Education* 9 (1975): 281-291.

Lasky, L. "An Exploration of Alternative Environmental Arrangements for Kindergarten Art Activity." Unpublished doctoral dissertation, Teachers College, Columbia University, 1972.

Linderman, E. W., and Herberholz, D. W. *Developing Artistic and Perceptual Awareness.* Dubuque, Iowa: William C. Brown, 1979.

Lowenfeld, V., and Brittain, W. L. *Creative and Mental Growth.* 6th ed. New York: Macmillan, 1975.

McCarthy, M., and Houston, J. P. *Fundamentals of Early Childhood Education.* Cambridge, Mass.: Winthrop Publishers, Inc., 1980.

McFee, J. K. "Art and Environmental Awareness." In *Commission on Art Education, Report of National Art Education Association.* Reston, Va.: National Art Education Association, 1977.

Madeja, S. S., ed. "The Arts, Cognition and Basic Skills." In *Second Yearbook on Research in Arts and Aesthetic Education.* Washington, D. C.: National Institute of Education, 1978.

Mussen, P. H. *The Psychological Development of the Child.* Englewood Cliffs, N.J.: Prentice-Hall, 1973.

Piaget, J. *The Psychology of Intelligence.* Totowa, N.J.: Littlefield, Adams & Co., 1972.

Randhawa, B. S., and Coffman, W. E., eds. *Visual Learning, Thinking, and Communication.* New York: Academic Press, 1978.

Reichenberg-Hackett, W. "Influence of Nursery Group Experience on Children's Drawings." *Psychological Reports* 14 no. 2 (April 1964): 433-434.

Robison, H. F. *Exploring Teaching in Early Childhood.* Boston: Allyn and Bacon, 1977.

Seefeldt, C. *Social Studies for the Preschool-Primary Child.* Columbus, Ohio: Merrill, 1977.

Silver, R. *Developing Cognitive Skills Through Art.* Baltimore, Md.: University Park Press, 1978.

Silver, R. "The Role of Art in the Conceptual Thinking, Adjustment and Aptitude of Deaf and Aphasic Children." Unpublished doctoral dissertation, Teachers College, Columbia University, 1966.

Spodek, B. *Teaching in the Early Years.* Englewood Cliffs, N.J.: Prentice-Hall, 1978.

6
Reaching Out to Other Expressive Arts

Creative adults in the arts are finally catching up with young children. On the contemporary arts scene, there is a striking movement toward multimedia artwork. Walk-in sculpture environments, a mix of live dance and film, actors moving into the audience to engage it in the drama—all are new ways to integrate the arts.

This exciting development may be new for sophisticated artists, but it is a familiar approach for young children. I think of five-year-old Maya, engrossed in her brilliant painting, first swinging her brush in broad curving sweeps across the paper, then dabbing with quick splotches of contrasting color. She steps back as if to survey her work. Instead, she breaks into swooping broad body movements, punctuated with quick little jabs into the air with her fingers. Both painting and dancing express her gaiety and freedom.

In this example, art leads a child into dance, but it is not a one-way street. It is just as likely that a child's spontaneous, expressive movement will lead her to form a piece of clay with a lovely sense of flow. As she runs her fingers over the cool, moist clay, she half chants, half sings,

> Loopey, loopey,
> scoopey,
> doopey,
> scoopey,
> doopey,
> doodie.

She has now expressed her ideas in movement, in art, and in poetry.

Young children naturally integrate arts unself-consciously—weaving back and forth among graphic arts, movement, dance, drama, music, and poetry in their expressive activities. Their expression in one art form stimulates greater expressiveness in other arts.

Through these channels for growing and learning, children bring information from the outside world. They *perceive* objects and events and interpret them in their own ways, trying to fit them into what they know so they make sense. Children work at making sense when they play, talk, dance, paint, or try to express what they are beginning to know about the outside world and what it means to them.

Making sense is the path to learning, one of the basic tasks for young children. They learn by making connections between earlier experiences and current experiences so that ideas become clearer, more focused, or more accurate.

Young children naturally integrate arts unself-consciously—weaving back and forth among graphic arts, movement, dance, drama, music, and poetry in their expressive activities.

Common aesthetic elements

Young children find no difficulty in learning through integrated arts. They are not yet hampered by the conventional labels used by adults to separate each art expression into closed pigeonholes. Children intuitively treat the arts as interrelated, which they are, because all the arts have important aesthetic elements in common. A few common elements of particular relevance to young children's experiences with the arts are color, pattern, line, space, rhythm, and contrast. Young children experience how art reaches out to the other creative arts through these common elements.

Color

Young children are fascinated by color in paints, crayons, felt pens, and found objects. They become absorbed in the mixtures of color and their magic changes as well as in the lightness and darkness of color. When children internalize their observations of color and its properties, they can transmute them to other purposes.

One early dawn, three-year-old Iver tried to convince his mother that he should not go back to sleep, saying, "But Mommy, the lightening is mixing with the darkening and it's almost daytime." Iver was connecting his experiences of light/dark with colorful word images—the beginnings of creative writing, more accurately described in young children as creating with words.

Pattern

Children's awareness of pattern in art, from later scribbling to schematic forms, can also be related to the songs they sing. They are captivated by the Moroccan folk song "Zum Gali Gali" (Dallin and Dallin 1972) and often exclaim gleefully, "You sing the same way two times; then you sing the new part two times,"—an accurate description of the song's pattern. It is not necessary to read music notation to discover the pattern of a song and how it goes up and down.

Children can also create their own sound patterns. These can be made of body sounds by clapping, clicking, beeping, and many more. They can be made with stones and bones and sticks and nails. Sound patterns can, of course, also be made with rhythm instruments, but growing sensitivity to sound patterns does not occur when everyone makes any old sound at the same time in an effort to drown out the accompanying record.

One interesting idea is to visualize various sound patterns on the chalkboard (Figure 23). It is easy to see how conducting these kinds of symbols could result in sounds that are percussive, sustained, sharp, moving from loud to soft, quivering, wailing, and from fast to slow to fast. One could draw innumerable other sound qualities.

Fig. 23. Sound patterns.

The teacher first indicates a sound picture and then conducts the sound pattern, but children quickly can add symbols and conduct imaginative sound patterns. Making these sound collages can be done successfully long before children can read conventional music notation and is, in fact, an experience on which to build later music reading (see McDonald 1979). Awareness of pattern in art extends to patterns in creative drama and creative movement, as well as music.

Line

Creative movement or dance especially displays a relationship to the element of line. When children are moving in a wiggly way or a twisting way or a floating way, they can be given a signal to freeze or hold by the striking of a gong or stopping a record. The teacher then appreciatively points out the different lines the body makes while it is held or frozen—the continuous curve from back toe through the body to the reaching, stretched fingers. The children can also make similar observations about each other's interesting body line designs in space. It is natural, then, to circle back from one's understanding of the body line to reaching, curving, twisting lines in clay or crayon or paint.

Space

When young children represent their art images in space, they tell us a great deal of how they feel about themselves and other people or objects in their lives. In Tamara's painting of her family, she placed her father prominently in the center, with herself and her mother on either side of him. She was touching her father, while her mother was separated by a space. Tamara's spacing of her family accurately revealed her feelings of closeness to her adored father compared with her feelings toward her mother whom she loved, but with less passion.

This emotional meaning of space is clearly matched when children engage in aspects of creative drama, particularly in pantomime. One can see the picture of pain in Kerry's face when he scrunches up to fit into an imaginary, too-tiny space. One can sense his feeling of bigness when he stretches to fill the tallest box in the world. When Dena tramples through the forest and uproots trees as strong elephants do, one can feel her affirming her power and confidence by her movement in space.

Children naturally respond to space in highly personal ways. Five-year-old Donna was elated by the vast cathedral space reaching to elongated stained glass windows. She exclaimed excitedly,

> I feel I'm flying way, way up to the window top.
> Way, way up, up, up,
> Flying like a bird.

Her spontaneous poem captured her sense of space and freedom. Six-year-old Oscar was cowed by that same expansive space, whispering, "It's scary; let's get out of here!" Although different, each child felt the impact of space and was able convincingly to dance out its personal meaning later.

Rhythm

The element of rhythm is most frequently associated with music, dance, and poetry, but it can be just as much a quality in art. We find it in repeated shapes, colors, and textures which flow in a directional path, and children's nature print designs. We also sense rhythm in their block structures of repeated patterns. We know rhythm unmistakably in the pulse of movement and music.

A four-year-old child feels important when the teacher tunes in to the rhythm of his gallop by matching it on a drum. The steady, driving pulse of the "Dakota Indian Work Song" (learned in the oral tradition by the author) as one sings, "To our work, we must go . . ." never fails to bring on some strong rhythmic accompaniment of clapping or slapping the floor. A natural development leads into rhythmically chopping trees as one type of work done in the forest while the work song goes on. As the song continues

> To the fields and to the rivers,
> To our work we go,
> To our work we go,

children capture the rhythmic pattern of paddling canoes and fishing.

It is one small step from this pantomime to that of painting the rhythm of flowing water. Seven-year-old children are often interested in learning some of the stylized rhythmic patterns of traditional Native American signs which tell stories about mountains, rivers, sun, and lightning in their weaving, pottery, bead work, and sand painting.

These few examples suggest how an awareness of rhythm links together experiences in art, music, movement, and the poetry of lyrics.

Contrast

The element of contrast provides one of the most exciting characteristics in all the arts. Sensitive teachers frequently help children become more aware of the power of contrast by pointing out how two colors next to each other make the shapes stand out. They comment on the roughly textured wings of a clay bird in contrast to its smooth head. Children appreciate the exaggerated features of "evil creature" puppets in contrast to the more subtle features of the heroes and heroines.

In music, songs that contain interesting contrast often become popular. "Loud March" (*Activity Song Book* 1949, p. 26) engages children in "Banging my pots and crashing my pans . . ." as they sing lustily and march loudly with instruments. They enjoy the dramatic contrast of the second verse:

> Up on my tiptoes, quiet as a kitten,
> nobody hears me, sh. . sh. . . . sh. . . . . . .

What can be more fun than walking in peanut butter contrasted with trying to walk up an icy hill? Or being a tightly closed umbrella, then a huge open umbrella on a windy day? Or, first being a powerful, prowling attacking lioness on the hunt and then, after eating, lolling about and playing with your romping cubs—just as real lions do?

There is something inherently satisfying in contrasting expression—almost as if the contrasts provide a balance that is lively rather than static, resulting in a sense of making things right in the end.

These six aesthetic elements apply in some distinctive form to all the arts. The examples of color, pattern, line, space, rhythm, and contrast as experienced through art, movement, sound, dance, music, and creative drama for young children will, it is hoped, confirm the concept that all the arts are interrelated in the lives of growing children.

Interweaving the arts in learning

Because common aesthetic elements can be found in all art forms, those who work with young children can gain confidence in providing a wide range of activities in integrated arts. We can think of experiences with a variety of materials and ideas and know, by identifying the key aesthetic elements, that the activities are worthwhile for enhancing the aesthetic awareness and creative expressiveness of children.

As teachers, we have the opportunity—and the obligation—to enhance children's natural modes of complex, integrated learning by fostering multichannel experiences in the arts. Fortunately, children give us the pattern and cues for learning through interweaving arts in their spontaneous play.

Spontaneous relationships

When young children first engage in airplane play, for example, they are the airplane, zooming around the room, dipping their extended wings, curving into a two-point landing before taking off again to their own cascading sounds of "vroom . . . . vroom . . . . . ." Movement, sound, and drama, expressed in line, form, and contrast, are integrated into one dramatic whole. Such spontaneous play could sometimes provide the basis for greater freedom in finger painting or preschematic painting or even scribbling by the very young child.

The same spontaneous interweaving of arts occurs with older children. A group of six-year-old children were building a rocket ship from a large cardboard barrel donated by a maintenance man. The children worked laboriously to saw an entry door and to solve the problem of attaching a nose cone. Intermittently, however, they slipped away from their construction tasks to become astronauts. Suddenly they were on Mars, bouncing along slowly, arms and legs akimbo, exclaiming about the funny people with pointed heads.

The observant teacher picked up this cue and used it with them later for a challenging, simple creative drama. She posed key questions to help them visualize character and action: Are the Martians bigger or smaller than the astronauts? Are they afraid? Anxious? Curious? Angry? Friendly? How do they show it? Do the astronauts invite the Martians to visit their rocket ship? How does the story end?

At another time, the teacher recorded an interview between an astronaut and a television news reporter. She typed the interview on a primary typewriter and several children illustrated the report. Many children could read the picture story; a few could also read the words.

The rocket then underwent further construction until the nose cone was secured, the entire structure painted and decorated, and antennae attached to the top.

The teacher's well-timed intervention, based on strong cues from the children, gave an added depth of meaning to their experience. It especially helped increase the children's sensitivity to how people feel in new situations or with people who are strange to them. The children also became more aware of how we talk with our actions, not just with our words. As the teacher showed clearly that she valued their productive activity, the children showed more persistence in solving their construction problems with the rocket in order to enjoy its use in extended dramatic play.

Planned relationships

Teachers can also initiate learning through the arts. A solid foundation on which to base plans for an integrated arts curriculum is the knowledge of how children develop and how adults can help them learn what they need for nurturing their own development.

We know that young children are learning to become better able to cope with life as they find it, to know about the world through their basic modes of sensory awareness and preoperational thinking, and to communicate with others and receive and understand communication from others.

Coping with life

As young children grow, they need to know about themselves as well as about other people. *How* children see themselves is crucial to their becoming worthy people—competent and deserving of appreciation and love. Children who feel worthy can learn to cope with limits, differences, and inevitable conflicts as they leave their narrow egocentric world for the larger social milieu. These children develop the confidence to explore, experiment, and be open in their contacts with other human beings.

Young children are generally spontaneous in activities that are eventually associated with the arts. Making fragments of music in the sounds they produce in dramatic play, they chant, hum, and play with words. Children exuberantly make patterns in space. They design forms with color and line, with blocks and beautiful junk. By presenting themselves through the arts, they see themselves more clearly.

Tabor learns something important about himself through his bold paint strokes or his thin, wavering lines. He learns more about himself when he puffs up and stalks like a big bear, or when he timidly tries to twirl, loses his balance, and sprawls awkwardly on the floor.

Children learn about themselves when they make choices in their art expressions, because all the arts necessitate choices. Four-year-old Tony realized that making choices can require self-affirmation. He had hesitantly begun to twist

Children learn about themselves when they make choices in their art expressions, because all the arts necessitate choices.

and turn, pretending he was a gathering storm. Almost in spite of himself, he was caught up in the drama of the storm, becoming more furious and wild in his rushing, whirling, flailing dance. The teacher, sensing its importance to Tony, asked if he wanted some music or sound to go with his storm. He did. She offered to play the drum and his friend suggested the tambourine, but Tony wanted neither. After some thought, he said, "Crumble the sandwich stuff (aluminum foil), then crumble it loud." The sound was perfect; it did not dominate his storm, but effectively supported it.

The risk that comes from making choices in the arts differs from a risk in response to a dare. It is a risk in response to oneself and to one's inner barometer of one's own courage at that moment. In the arts, one chooses how much of a risk to take. For example, Tony's teacher helped him expand his expression by leading him to the related area of sound, but she did it in such a way as to keep the situation open enough for Tony to make the choice. Tony affirmed himself and his unique humanness in four-year-old terms.

Learning about the world

Learning about oneself is intertwined with learning about the world of people, objects, and events. Such learning mainly takes place through the processes of sensory awareness, perceptual awareness, association, and generalization. The expressive arts help in these processes of cognitive learning about the world.

The arts deepen children's sensory awareness through the use of their natural curiosity. Their sensory awareness is nourished by teachers who help them focus on the variations and contrasts in the environment: the feel and look of smooth bark and rippling rough bark, the heaviness of rock and the lightness of pumice stone, the feathery leaf and the leathery leaf, the slippery marble and the sticky tar. The rumble and screech of a subway taking a curve, the whisper of leaves against a window pane, the purr of a well-tuned motor, the shattering clap of thunder. All these are grist for expression in the arts, in poetry, in movement and sound, and in two- and three-dimensional art forms.

Children exploring with paint, crayon, wood, clay, or found materials are faced with unlimited possibilities to nourish their perceptual awareness. An alert and caring teacher observes the joy of discovery with a knowing smile, or asks the question that leads to further exploration.

What might children perceive about paint? It glides; it drags; it blobs; it spills; it spreads magically on wet paper and in water; it can be made lighter, darker, more intense, less intense; it can mix to make new colors; and it can swallow up all the colors to make that special shade of brown known as "yucky!"

What might children perceive about the surrounding kaleidoscope of moving images? They notice the smooth gliding and sudden dips of the sea gull, the swishing of the puppy's tail, the rhythmic semaphoric pattern of a police officer directing traffic, a skater's awkward sprawling fall on the ice. In their own bodies, through their kinesthetic senses, they perceive these images in movement.

In addition to providing the materials for sensory and perceptual awareness, teachers of young children support them as they begin to make associations. Children develop important understandings through associations: The smaller drums have higher sounds than the bigger ones. On an autoharp, the shorter strings have higher sounds than the longer ones. When the clay is too hard, it needs more water. When there is too much water in the playdough, it becomes too sticky. The teacher purposefully facilitates such associations. Eventually, these associations cluster together in children's thinking, and the children reach for a generalization.

Even very young children struggle with the sophisticated step of thinking known as generalizing. Their attempts at generalizing often seem funny to adults but are actually quite reasonable for their stage of development. As one three-year-old girl said to the student teacher who was at least twenty years younger than her cooperating teacher, "You must be the oldest teacher in the room because you have the biggest feet!" She had arrived at the generalization bigger is older.

Some generalizations about the movement of animals are, unfortunately, stereotypes with no basis in awareness or perception. One thinks of the generations of young children who have been given a false image of the elephant as a heavy, awkward, lumbering beast. People in India, Sri-Lanka, and parts of Africa who live with elephants have a vastly different perception of them. The generalized symbol for the elephant in Indian dance is that of delicate waving ears and the smooth undulations of its flexible trunk. The metaphor for an elegant, graceful woman in India refers to her as "an elephant-gaited woman"—a complimentary generalization.

Young children draw generalizations from their personal lives. One can appreciate the efforts of six-year-old Cathy in her group which was having problems developing a creative drama. In the story, a little boy' longed desperately for a cat of his own. His mother refused to allow it. The drama was floundering when the little boy kept repeating, "I want it," and the mother parried with a repetitive "no." Finally, Cathy came up with a pertinent generalization and a solution for moving the drama forward. She cued the mother, saying, "If you want him to understand why you don't want a cat in the house, you have to give him good reasons. You can't just say 'no.' Mothers have reasons."

The arts alone provide limited fertile ground for basic cognitive learning. Without question, however, the arts are particularly effective in nourishing cognitive processes through sensory awareness, perceptual awareness, association, and generalization. On the other hand, the arts do nothing for rote learning and vice versa.

Communicating

Learning to become better able to cope and learning about the world are connected with young children's third task: learning to communicate. Except for unusual circumstances, in their first two or three years, all children learn to speak and amass a surprisingly large vocabulary. Incredibly, they construct rules for their home language which resemble adult rules but without as many aggravating exceptions.

It is efficient to code concepts with words and be able to have a vocabulary with which to communicate. How do these words gather meaning? Concepts of up and down, beside, behind, in front of, under, and over are all spatial terms which are learned in relation to a child's own body. They are learned by a body in motion, through movement.

In dance, the arms swing over the head, sideways, and down. Aroundness means twirling around, spinning around, rolling the head around, galloping around the room, and wrapping one's arms around oneself. Then, in constructions, putting the wool around a frame; printing small shapes around the big, central one; wrapping the skirt around the stick puppet. This is aroundness in a fuller way.

The vocabulary learned through action needs to be expressed so that a child can communicate verbally. The process of creating with words has its roots in verbal manipulation and experimentation. Teachers recognize the difficulty some young children have communicating with words in school. In such situations, teachers search for ways to encourage children's verbal communication. Some of the most successful breakthroughs occur when the teacher offers silent children puppets who can talk to more verbal puppets. Under the safety of a paper bag mask, or protected by the security of a handmade puppet, many nursery or kindergarten children talk, for the first time in school, as the character of a puppet.

Under imaginative teacher guidance, the interweaving arts of puppetry, movement, and creative drama can extend basic vocabulary building into the art of creating with words. Children are encouraged to communicate in colorful language and poetic expression. Their standard and nonstandard words are sometimes startling in their beauty, especially when they arise from meaningful experiences.

> A lullaby is a quiet song your
> mother sings to you when you go to
> sleep—so you won't be afraid.
> (4-year-old child)

> (while feeling their bare feet)
> They're soft, boney, bumpy, lumpy . . .
> Big fat bumpy lump . . .
> Yucky, stinkey, feet!
> (4-year-old children)

> (upon hearing Debussy)
> I felt like an angel was in my head.
> There was a dream in my eyes.
> (5-year-old child)

(while feeling a rabbit)
A rabbit feels like cotton when it first grows.
Like my newborn cousin's hand.
(5-year-old child)

As quiet as a floor when no one
is walking on it.
(5-year-old child)

Angora wool is soft, hairy spaghetti.
(6-year-old child)

As angry as when steam comes out
of my ears, your ears boil, and your
face gets red.
(6-year-old child)

The following incident about children and bridges underscores the impact of direct, active experience on expressive communication. In a school near the Brooklyn Bridge, some of the kindergarten children became interested in bridges. The teacher secured some fine photographs of this beautifully designed bridge, and from them the children dictated this story: "This is the Brooklyn Bridge. It is big." Then, with considerable prompting from the teacher, they concluded, "It has stones."

The next day the teacher took the children for a walk the whole length of that dramatic bridge. Here is some of the language in their later dictation:

about the bridge—"It goes up, up, up till my neck hurts. It's shaky. It's
              rumbly."
about the sea gulls—"They swished and floated. They swooped. They
              scoopey, scooped."
about the water
under the bridge—"It spangled!"

When the children's creative writing was used later as the basis for their creative movement, all the images, whether of the bridge, the water, the sea gulls, or the ships, had a sense of power and bigness that was also strangely contained by a rather slow, underlying rhythm.

The bridge they built with blocks was much larger than any previous block structure. The children searched for ways to attach parallel strands of cord to recall the distinctive silhouette of the real bridge. Large rolls of wrapping paper were painstakingly painted to represent the river. For days, various boat-like objects were added to the river site. It was not easy for the children to dismantle their complex structure at the end of the week, but janitorial necessity prevailed.

The Brooklyn Bridge saga engaged most of the children in the group at one time or another in different ways. Some children made their entry through creating with words; others were attracted by the swooping of the sea gulls expressed in creative movement. A few became involved primarily through block building. Others took a first step by painting the river. However, as the week progressed, the children moved out beyond their initial entry through one of the arts into participation in other, interweaving arts.

Children as well as adults prefer to move from a base of security and confidence into less comfortable or less charted spheres of expression. A knowledgeable and aware teacher plans how best to lead children from their preferred medium of expression into other, related channels of aesthetic creation.

Do we need *all* the creative arts in the curriculum for young children? If we want children to develop their powers of communication, to know about the world, to know about themselves and other people, and thus to grow in humanness—the answer is a resounding **yes.**

References

Dallin, L., and Dallin, L. "Zum Gali Gali." Dubuque, Iowa: William C. Brown, 1972.

"Loud March." *Activity Song Book.* New York: Young Peoples Records, Inc., 1949.

McDonald, D. T. *Music in Our Lives: The Early Years.* Washington, D. C.: National Association for the Education of Young Children, 1979.

Mukerji, R. "Growing Together Through the Arts." *Today's Education* 69, no. 2 (April-May 1980): 443-463.

Appendix A
Sources of Free and Inexpensive Materials

Source	Materials
Aircraft manufacturers	Scrap parts, plywood, aluminum
Art materials manufacturers	Sample products
Book shops	Damaged books, outdated magazines
Cabinetmakers	Sawdust, wood shavings, laminated cutouts, wood turnings, scraps
Contractors	Scrap building materials
Cosmetic manufacturers	Damaged packaging materials
Department stores	Gift catalogs, boxes, wrapping paper, tissue, ribbons, corrugated and Styrofoam™ packaging items
Drug stores	Pictures from displays, leaflets, discarded plastic bottles and jars, lids, droppers
Dry cleaners and laundries	Shirt cardboards, packing materials, wire hangers, plastic bags, hanger cardboards
Duplicating firms and printers	Cardboard cylinders from copy machines, paper
Fabric manufacturers and shops	Remnants of fabric and trimmings
Florists	Dried flowers, bits of ribbon, scrap Styrofoam™, dropped leaves, seed pods
Garment manufacturers	Empty spools, fabric scraps, buttons, trimmings
Government agencies	Posters, maps, illustrated brochures
Hardware and paint stores	Wallpaper sample books, tile samples, paint chips, screws, nuts, bolts, plastic and metal fittings
Junk yards/house wreckers	Furniture legs, drawer pulls, door knobs, hinges, parts of appliances, gears, wheels, pulleys

Knitting mills	Yarn cones, yarn samples
Lumber yards	Doweling, scrap lumber and hardboard, sawdust, shavings, damaged bricks and cement blocks, trim scraps
Metal spinning companies	Scrap turnings and shavings
Newspapers	Paper roll ends, ink
Paper manufacturers	Irregular products, samples
Plumbers	Wire, tiles, pieces of pipe
Public relations departments	Samples of products
Rug manufacturers	Pieces of carpet
Seed companies	Catalogs
Shoe and pocketbook manufacturers	Scraps of leather and plastics, laces, fittings
Stationers	Old greeting cards, paper, ink
Supermarkets	Berry baskets, fruit crates, molded cardboard and Styrofoam™ trays, cartons, packaging and display items
Telephone and power companies	Excess colored wire, large spools
Tile manufacturers	Seconds of tile in bulk
Window shade companies	Shade cutoffs, pieces of rollers
Wine and liquor stores	Wooden wine crates, cartons, ribbons, gift paper, display items
Your home and neighborhood	Empty boxes, containers, tubes, knitting and sewing cast-offs, foils, plastics and other package wrappers, bits of string, leaves, twigs, grasses, seed pods, tree bark, pebbles

Appendix B
Children's Books about Art

Learning about colors, forms, and textures

Ehlert, L. *Planting a Rainbow*. New York: Harcourt Brace Jovanovich, 1988.

Hoban, T. *Spirals, Curves, Fanshapes & Lines*. New York: Greenwillow Books, 1992.

Hutchins, P. *Changes, Changes*. New York: Macmillan, 1971.

Jonas, A. *Color Dance*. Boston: Little, Brown, 1992.

Lionni, L. *Little Blue and Little Yellow*. New York: Astor-Honor, 1949.

Lobel, A. *The Great Blueness and Other Predicaments*. New York: Harper & Row, 1968.

Provenson, M., and Provenson, A. *Roses are Red. Are Violets Blue?* New York: Random House, 1973.

Rogers, P. *The Shapes Game*. New York: Henry Holt, 1990.

Shaw, C.G. *It Looks Like Spilled Milk*. New York: Harper & Row, 1947.

Showers, P. *Find Out by Touching*. Illustrated by Robert Galster. New York: Crowell, 1961.

Walsh, E.S. *Mouse Paint*. New York: Harcourt Brace Jovanovich, 1990.

Wolff, R.J. *Seeing Red*. New York: Charles Scribner's Sons, 1968.

Yenawine, P., and Museum of Modern Art. *Series on Modern Art. Colors; Lines; Shapes; Stories*. New York: Delacorte Press, 1991.

Learning about artists and their artworks

Abby Aldrich Rockefeller Folk Art Center. *The Folk Art Counting Book*. New York: Abrams, 1991.

Bjork, C. *Linnea in Monet's Garden*. Illustrated by Lena Anderson. New York: R & S Books, 1985.

Blizzard, G. *Come Look With Me*. Charlottesville, VA: Thomasson-Grant, 1991, 1992.

Brown, L., and Brown, M. *Visiting the Art Museum*. New York: EP Dutton, 1986.

Chermayeff, I., and Chermayeff, J.C. *First Words*. New York: Henry N. Abrams, 1990.

Cummings, P. *Talking with Artists*. New York: Bradbury, 1992.

Everett, G. *Li'l Sis and Uncle Willie*. New York: Rizzoli, 1992.

Goffstein, M.B. *Lives of the Artists*. New York: Harper & Row, 1983.

Holmes, B. *Enchanted Worlds: Pictures to Grow Up With*. New York: Universal Press, 1979.

Holmes, B. *Creatures of Paradise: Pictures to Grow Up With*. New York: University Press, 1980.

Kesselman, W., & Cooney, B. *Emma*. New York: Doubleday, 1980.

Koch, K., and Farerell, K. *Talking to the Sun: An Illustrated Anthology of Poems for Young People*. New York: Henry Holt, 1991.

Lawrence, J. *Harriet and the Promised Land*. New York: Simon & Schuster Books for Young Readers, 1993.

Mayers, F. *ABC, The Museum of Fine Arts*. Boston: Museum of Fine Arts, 1991.

Mayhew, J. *Katie's Picture Show*. New York: Bantam Books, 1989.

Micklethwait, L. *A Child's Book of Art: Great Pictures, First Words*. London: Dorling-Kindersley, 1993.

Micklethwait, L. *I Spy: An Alphabet in Art*. New York: Greenwillow Books, 1992.

Roalf, P. *Looking at Paintings (series). Landscapes*. New York: Hyperion Books for Children, 1992.

Strand, M. *Rembrandt Takes a Walk.* New York: Clarkson N. Potter, 1987.

Zadrzynaka, E. *The Girl with a Watering Can.* New York: Chameleon Books, 1989.

Zhensun, A., and Low, A. *A Young Painter: The Life and Paintings of Wang Yani, China's Extraordinary Artist.* New York: Scholastic, 1991.

Yenawine, P., and Museum of Modern Art. *Series on Modern Art. Colors; Lines; Shapes; Stories.* New York: Delacorte Press, 1991.

Learning about the art of many cultures

Baylor, B. *When Clay Sings.* New York: Charles Scribner's Sons, 1987.

Brown, M. *Shadow.* New York: Charles Scribner's Sons, 1991.

Cretan, G.Y. *Me, Myself, and I.* Illustrated by Don Bognese. New York: Morrow, 1969.

de Paola, T. *The Legend of the Indian Paintbrush.* New York: Putnam & Grosser, 1991.

Demi. *Liang and the Magic Paintbrush.* New York: Henry Holt, 1980.

Ehlert, L. *Moon Rope, Un Lago a la Luna.* San Diego/New York: Harcourt Brace Jovanovich, 1992.

Esterman, M.M. *A Fish That's a Box.* Arlington, VA: Great Ocean Publishers, 1990.

Garza, C.L. *Family Pictures, Cuadros de Familia.* San Francisco: Children's Book Press, 1990.

Grossman, V., and Long, S. *Ten Little Rabbits.* San Francisco: Chronicle Books, 1991.

McDermott, G. *The Magic Tree.* New York: Holt, Rinehart & Winston, 1973.

Miles, M. *Annie and the Old One.* Illustrated by Peter Parnall. Boston: Little, Brown, 1985.

Ringgold, F. *Tar Beach.* New York: Crown, 1991.

Sullivan, C., ed. *Children of Promise.* New York: Henry N. Abrams, 1991.

Seeing the world with the eyes of the artist

Carini, E. *Take Another Look.* Englewood Cliffs, N.J.: Prentice-Hall, 1970.

Cohen, M., & Hoban, L. *No Good in Art.* New York: Greenwillow, 1980.

dePaola, T. *The Art Lesson.* New York: Putnam, 1989.

Ernst, L.C. *Hamilton's Art Show.* New York: Lothrop, 1986.

Isadora, R. *The Pirates of Bedford Street.* New York: Greenwillow, 1988.

Leen, N. *Taking Pictures.* New York: Holt, Rinehart & Winston, 1977.

Lionni, L. *Matthew's Dream.* New York: Alfred A. Knopf, 1991.

Lund, D.H. *The Paint Box Sea.* Illustrated by Symeon Shimin. New York: McGraw-Hill, 1973.

Some outstanding illustrators of children's books

Because artistic books have a strong impact on the aesthetic development of their readers, we have selected a number of artists whose illustrations of children's literature are consistently outstanding. The Caldecott Award is a reliable guide for selecting beautifully illustrated children's books.

Adrienne Adams	Diane Dillon	Frane Léssac	Maurice Sendak
Molly Bang	Leo Dillon	Arnold Lobel	Uri Shulevitz
Marcia Brown	Roger Duvoisin	Robert McCloskey	Lane Smith
Nancy Burkett	Richard Egielski	Beni Montresor	Chris Van Allsburg
Virginia Burton	Lois Ehlert	Dav Pilkey	Lynd Ward
Eric Carle	Marie Hall Ets	Leo Politi	David Weisner
Victoria Chess	Wanda Gag	Alice Provenson	Brian Wildsmith
Barbara Cooney	Trina Shart Hyman	Martin Provenson	Garth Williams
Alexandra Day	Ezra Jack Keats	Faith Ringgold	Taro Yashima

146

Appendix C
For Further Reading

Children, art, and art education

Alexander, K. *Spectra Program (grades 1–6).* Menlo Park, CA: Dale Seymour Publications, 1987.

Alland, A. *Playing with Form: Children Draw in Six Cultures.* New York: Columbia University Press, 1983.

Anderson, F.E. *Art for All the Children.* 2nd ed. Springfield, IL: Charles C. Thomas, 1992.

Anderson, T. "Talking about Art with Children: From Theory to Practice." *Art Education* 39 (1986): 5–8.

Arnheim, R. *Art and Visual Perception: The New Version.* Berkeley, CA: University of California Press, 1974.

Barnes, R. *Teaching Art to Young Children.* Boston: Allen & Unwin, 1987.

Briere, M. *Art Image, 1–6.* Champlain, NY: Art Image Publications, 1989.

Brown, E.V. "Development Characteristics of Clay Figures Made by Children from Age 3 through Age 11." *Studies in Art Education* 16 (1976): 45–53.

Carothers, J.T., and Gardner, H. "When Children's Drawings Become Art: The Emergence of Aesthetic Production and Perception." *Developmental Psychology* 15 (1979): 570–80.

Castrup, J., Ain, E., and Scott, R. "Art Skills of Preschool Children." *Studies in Art Education* 13 (1972): 62–69.

Cecil, N.L., & Lauritzen, P. *Literacy and the Arts for the Integrated Classroom.* NY: Longman, 1994.

Chapman, L.H. *Adventures in Art, 1–6.* Worcester, MA: Davis Productions, 1994.

Cherry, C. *Creative Art for the Developing Child.* Belmont, CA: Fearon, 1972.

Clare, S.M. "The Drawings of Preschool Children: A Longitudinal Case Study and Four Experiments." *Studies in Art Education* 29 (1988): 211–21.

Clemens, S.G. "Art in the Classroom: Making Every Day Special." *Young Children* 46, no. 2 (1991): 4–11.

Clement, R. *The Art Teacher's Handbook.* London: Hutchinson, 1985.

Cocking, R.R., and Copple, C.E. "Change through Exposure to Others: A Study of Children's Verbalizations As They Draw" in *Piagetian Theory and Its Implications for the Helping Professions (Proceedings, Eighth Interdisciplinary Conference, Vol II),* ed. by M.K. Poulsen and G.I. Lubin. University Park, CA: University of Southern California Press, 1979.

Colbert, C. "Status of the Visual Arts in Early Education." *Art Education* 37, no. 4 (1984) 28–31.

Colbert, C., and Taunton, M. *Discover Art Kindergarten.* Worcester, MA: Davis Publications, 1990.

Cole, E., and Schaefer, C. "Can Young Children Be Art Critics?" *Young Children* 45, no. 2 (1990): 33–38.

Coles, R. *Their Eyes Meeting the World: The Drawings and Paintings of Children,* ed. by M. Sartor. Boston: Houghton Mifflin, 1992.

Day, M., and Hurwitz, A. *Children and Their Art.* 5th ed. Orlando, FL: Harcourt Brace Jovanovich, 1991.

Dyson, A.H. "Appreciate the Drawing and Dictating of Young Children." *Young Children* 43, no. 3 (1988): 25–32.

Dyson, A.H. "Symbol Makers, Symbol Weavers: How Young Children Link Play, Pictures, and Print." *Young Children* 45, no. 2 (1990): 50–57.

Edwards, C.P., Gandini, L., and Forman, G. *The Hundred Languages of Children: The Reggio Emilia Approach to Early Childhood Education.* Norwood, NJ: Ablex, 1993.

Edwards, L.C., and Nabors, M.L. "The Creative Arts Process: What It Is and What It Is Not." *Young Children* 48, no. 3 (1993): 77–81.

Eisner, E. ed. *The Arts, Human Development and Education.* Berkeley, CA: McCutchan, 1976.

Feeney, S., and Moravcik, E. "A Thing of Beauty: Aesthetic Development in Young Children." *Young Children* 42, no. 6 (1987): 7–15.

Fein, S. *Heidi's Horse.* Pleasant Hill, CA: Exerod Press, 1976.

Feinburg, S.G. "Conceptual Content and Spatial Characteristics in Boys' and Girls' Drawings of Fighting and Helping." *Studies in Art Education* 18 (1977): 68–72.

Freeman, N.H. *Strategies of Representation in Young Children.* London: Academic Press, 1980.

Freeman, N.H., and Cox, M.V., eds. *Visual Order: The Development of Pictorial Representation.* Cambridge: Cambridge University Press, 1985.

Fucigna, C., Ives, K.C., and Ives, W. "Art for Toddlers: A Developmental Approach." *Young Children* 37, no. 3 (1982): 45–52.

Gallas, K. "Arts as Epistemology: Enabling Children to Know What They Know." *Harvard Educational Review* 61, no. 1 (1991): 40–50.

Gardner, H. *Art Education and Human Development.* Los Angeles: Getty Center for Education in the Arts, 1990.

Gardner, H. *Art, Mind, and Brain: A Cognitive Approach to Creativity.* New York: Basic Books, 1982.

Gardner, H. *Artful Scribbles.* New York: Basic Books, 1980.

Gardner, H. *The Arts and Human Development: A Psychological Study of the Artistic Process.* New York: John Wiley and Sons, 1973.

Gardner, H., and Wolf, D. "The Symbolic Products of Early Childhood" in *Curiosity, Imagination, and Play,* ed. by D. Gorlitz and J. Wohlwill. Hillsdale, NJ: Lawrence Erlbaum, 1987.

Garritson, J.S. *Childarts: Integrating Curriculum Through the Arts.* Menlo Park, CA: Addison-Wesley Publishing Co., 1979.

Gearhart, M., and Newman, D. "Learning to Draw a Picture: The Social Context of an Individual Activity." *Discourse Processes* 3 (1980): 169–184.

Golomb, C. *The Child's Creation of a Pictorial World.* Berkeley, CA: University of California Press, 1929.

Goodnow, J. *Children Drawing.* Cambridge, MA: Harvard University Press, 1977.

Grossman, E. "Effects of Instructional Experience in Clay Modeling Skills on Modeled Human Figure Representation in Preschool Children." *Studies in Art Education* 22, no. 1 (1980): 51–59.

Haskell, L.L. *Art in the Early Childhood Years.* Columbus, OH: Merrill, 1979.

Heard, D. "Children's Drawing Styles." *Studies in Art Education* 29, no. 4 (1988): 222–31.

Henley, D.R. *Exceptional Children, Exceptional Art.* Worcester, MA: Davis Publications, 1992.

Herberholz, B., & Hanson, L. *Early Childhood Art,* 5th ed. Dubuque, IA: Brown & Benchmark, 1995.

Hill, D. *Mud, Sand, and Water.* Washington, DC: National Association for the Education of Young Children, 1977.

Hubbard, R. *Authors of Pictures, Draughtsmen of Words.* Portsmouth, NH: Heinemann, 1989.

Hubbard, R. "Transferring Images: Not Just Glued on the Page." *Young Children* 42, no. 2 (1987): 60–67.

Johnson, N. "Children's Meanings about Art." *Studies in Art Education* 23, no. 3 (1982): 61–67.

Kellogg, R., and O'Dell, S. *The Psychology of Children's Art.* Palo Alto, CA: Mayfield Publishing Co., 1967.

Korzenik, D. "Socialization and Drawing." *Art Education* 32, no. 1 (1979): 26–29.

Kramer, E. *Childhood and Art Therapy.* New York: Schocken Books, 1980.

Lark-Horovitz, B., Lewis, H., and Luca, M. *Understanding Children's Art for Better Teaching.* 2nd ed. Columbus, OH: Charles E. Merrill, 1973.

Leeds, J.A. "Teaching and the Reasons for Making Art." *Art Education* 39 (1986): 17–21.

London, P. *Step Outside: Community-Based Art Education.* Portsmouth, NH: Heinemann, 1994.

Mattera, J. "Arts Are Basic: More Than a Philosophy." *School Arts* 79, no. 9 (May 1980): 50-51.

Matthews, J. "Children's Drawings: Are Young Children Really Scribbling?" *Early Child Development and Care* 18 (1984): 1-39.

Mukerji, R., and Rice, S. eds. *Children Are Centers for Media.* Washington, DC: Association for Childhood Education International, 1973.

Parsons, M.J. *How We Understand Art: A Cognitive Developmental Account of Aesthetic Experience.* New York: Cambridge University Press, 1987.

Parsons, M., Johnston, M., and Durham, R. "Developmental Stages in Children's Aesthetic Responses." *Journal of Aesthetic Education* 15, no. 1 (1981): 83-104.

Read, H. *Education Through Art.* New York: Pantheon, 1974.

Rosario, J., and Collazo, E. "Aesthetic Codes in Context: An Exploration in Two Preschool Classrooms." *Journal of Aesthetic Education* 15, no. 1 (1981): 71-84.

Schirrmacher, R. *Art and Creative Development for Young Children.* Albany, NY: Delmar Publishers, 1988.

Schirrmacher, R. "Talking With Children About Their Art." *Young Children* 41, no. 5 (1986): 3-7.

Sharp, P. "Aesthetic Response in Early Education." *Art Education* 29 (1976): 25-28.

Skeen, P., Garner, A.P., and Cartwright, S. *Woodworking for Young Children.* Washington, DC: National Association for the Education of Young Children, 1984.

Smilansky, S. Hagan, J., and Lewis, H. *Clay in the Classroom: Helping Children Develop Cognitive and Affective Skills for Learning.* New York: Teachers College Press, 1988.

Smith, N.R. "Drawing Conclusions: Do Children Draw from Observation?" *Art Education* 36, no. 3 (1983): 22-25.

Smith, N.R. *Experience and Art (Teaching Children to Paint).* 2nd ed., with C. Fucigna, M. Kennedy, and L. Lord. New York: Teachers College Press, 1993.

Smith, N.R., and Fucigna, C. "Drawing Systems in Children's Pictures: Contour and Form." *Visual Arts Research* 14, no. 1 (1988): 66-76.

Sparling, J.J., and Sparling, M.C. "How to Talk to a Scribbler" in *Exploring Early Childhood,* ed. by M. Kaplan-Sarnoff and R. Yablins-Magid. New York: Macmillan, 1981.

Tarr, P. "More Than Movement: Scribbling Reassessed." *Visual Arts Research* 16, no. 1 (1990): 83-89.

Taunton, M. "Aesthetic Responses of Young Children to the Visual Arts: A Review of the Literature." *Journal of Aesthetic Education* 16, no. 3 (1982): 93-109.

Taunton, M. "Reflective Dialogue in the Art Classroom: Focusing on the Art Process." *Art Education* (Jan. 1984): 15-16.

Taunton, M., and Colbert, C. "Artistic and Aesthetic Development: Considerations for Early Childhood Educators." *Childhood Education* 61, no. 1 (1984): 55-63.

Thompson, C. *Art Image Preschool* (5 vols.). Champlain, NY: Art Image Publications, 1994.

Thompson, C.M. "I Make a Mark: The Significance of Young Children's Talk about Their Art." *Early Childhood Research Quarterly* 5 (1990): 215-32.

Thompson, C.M., and Bales, S. "Michael Doesn't Like My Dinosaurs: Conversations in a Preschool Art Class." *Studies in Art Education* 33, no. 1 (1991): 43-55.

Winner, E. *Invented Worlds: The Psychology of the Arts.* Cambridge, MA: Harvard University Press, 1982.

Winner, E. "Where Pelicans Kiss Seals." *Psychology Today* (Aug. 1972): 25-26, 30-35.

Wolf, D., and Davis-Perry, M. "From End-Points to Repertoires: Some New Conclusions about Drawing Development." *Journal of Aesthetic Education* 22, no. 1 (1988): 17-34.

Zurmuehlen, M. *Studio Art: Praxis, Symbol, Presence.* Reston, VA: National Art Education Association, 1990.

Art processes

Alkema, C.J. *Puppet Making*. New York: Sterling Publishing, 1976.

Blackburn, G. *Illustrated Basic Carpentry*. New York: Van Nostrand Reinhold, 1972.

Blau, R., Brady, E., Bucher, I, Hiteshew, B., Zavitovsky, A., and Zavitovsky, D. *Activities for School-Age Child Care*. Washington, DC: National Association for the Education of Young Children, 1977.

Daniels, H., and Turner, S. *Simple Printmaking with Children*. New York: Van Nostrand Reinhold, 1972.

Fiarotta, P., and Fiarotta, N. *The You and Me Heritage Tree*. New York: Workman Publishing Co., 1976.

Grater, M. *Paper People*. New York: Tapling Publishing, 1970.

Grummer, A.E. *Paper by Kids*. New York: Macmillan, 1990.

Grummer, A.E. *Tin Can Papermaking: Recycle for Earth and Art*. Appleton, WI: Gregory Marekin, 1992.

Hanford, R.T. *Puppets and Puppeteering*. New York: Drake Publishers, 1976.

Hasten, I., and Frischman, R. *Curling, Coiling and Quilling*. New York: Sterling Publishing, 1973.

Holter, P. *Photography Without a Camera*. New York: Van Nostrand Reinhold, 1972.

Johnson, P. *Literacy through the Book Arts*. Portsmouth, NH: Heinemann, 1993.

Kampman, L. *Creating with Colored Paper*. New York: Van Nostrand Reinhold, 1967.

Kampman, L. *Creating with Crayons*. New York: Van Nostrand Reinhold, 1967.

Kampman, L. *Creating with Found Objects*. New York: Van Nostrand Reinhold, 1971.

Kampman, L. *Creating with Puppets*. New York: Van Nostrand Reinhold, 1971.

Langstaff, N., and Sproul, A. *Exploring with Clay*. Washington, DC: Association for Childhood Education International, 1979.

Latshaw, G. *Puppetry, the Ultimate Disguise*. New York: Richards Rosen Press, 1978.

Linderman, M. *Art in the Elementary School: Drawing, Painting, and Creating for the Classroom*. Dubuque, IA: Brown & Benchmark, 1990.

Lorrimer, B. *Creative Papier-Mâché*. New York: Watson Gupthill, 1971.

Newsome, A.J. *Cork and Wood Crafts*. New York: Lion Press, 1970.

Ross, L. *Scrap Puppets*. New York: Holt, Rinehart & Winston, 1978.

Rothenberg, P. *Complete Book of Ceramics*. New York: Crown, 1972.

Seville, R. *Beginning Arts and Crafts*. New York: Drake Publishers, 1971.

Silberstein-Storfer, M. *Doing Art Together*. New York: Simon & Schuster, 1982.

Sunset Books and Sunset Magazine, ed. *Ceramics*. Menlo Park, CA: Lane Books, 1973.

Tong, G. *Modeling with Self-hardening Clay*. New York: Van Nostrand Reinhold, 1969.

Topal, C.W. *Children and Painting*. Worcester, MA: Davis Productions, 1992.

Topal, C.W. *Children, Clay and Sculpture*. Worcester, MA: Davis Productions, 1983.

Wiseman, A. *Making Things*. Boston: Little, Brown, *Book I*, 1967; *Book II*, 1975.

Wolf, A.D. "Art Postcards—Another Aspect of Your Aesthetics Program?" *Young Children* 45, no. 2 (1990): 39–43.

Periodicals

Art Education
The National Art Education Association
1916 Association Dr.
Reston, VA 22091

Arts and Activities
591 Camino de la Reina,
Suite 200
San Diego, CA 92108

Journal of Aesthetic Education
University of Illinois Press
1325 Oak St.
Champaign, IL 61820

School Arts
Davis Publications
50 Portland St.
Worcester, MA 01608

Studies in Art Education
The National Art Education Association
1916 Association Dr.
Reston, VA 22091

Appendix D
Ideas for Using This Book with a Workshop or Class

Here are some ideas that we have found effective in working with classes or workshops to encourage members' involvement and deepen their understanding of various aspects of young children's development and experiences in art. We anticipate that you will develop your own variations on these ideas and that they will spark many new possibilities.

Chapter 1—Young Children Need Art
Ask students or workshop participants to write a brief anecdotal record of a child engaged in an art activity. Divided into groups, participants can share their anecdotal records and determine which of the values listed on page 4 are reflected in the children's behavior.

Chapter 2—Graphic Activity of Young Children: Development and Creativity
Participants are asked to bring samples of children's paintings and drawings with the child's age noted on the back. Display these examples without identifying the ages of the artists. Using the indicators of stages of development, as described in Chapter 2, participants estimate the stage of development of each child's work and the probable age of the child. Members are often surprised when they compare their estimates with the actual ages of the children. When conducting such a workshop for parents, we advise not including drawings by their own children.

Chapter 3—Fostering Creativity
1. Each participant writes an anecdotal observation record of a child who is using self-chosen art materials. Members share their records in small groups. In the context of the description of the creative process in this chapter, they identify the steps through which each child proceeded with the project.

2. If time is available, divide the workshop schedule so the members participate in two types of art experiences—one in which they replicate a model and one in which they use comparable materials in their own individual ways. For example, participants first could be asked to copy a clay snowman made from three graded-size spheres. Then they have the opportunity to model the same quantity of clay as they wish. Participants evaluate both experiences in terms of the steps in the creative process and the value of the experiences for individual creativity and learning as described in Chapter 3.

3. Workshops in which parents or teachers make items for the program, such as easels, supply shelves, or scissors racks, provide an opportunity to initiate a discussion about the creative process.

Chapter 4—The Art Program

Several types of hands-on workshops can be arranged using this chapter as a source of information about art processes.

1. Ask participants to bring a variety of found materials, such as those listed on page 34, and group people according to the items they plan to make, e.g., instruments, other learning games, or assemblages.

2. Focus on a single activity such as printmaking, woodwork, or making puppets. Members first read Chapter 4 and then decide which process and materials to use.

3. Focus on one of the three major categories in Chapter 4 (applying, forming, interlacing) for a series of workshops. Each participant selects one or more processes from the selected category. If the focus is applying, for example, some participants could draw with crayons or chalk, some fingerpaint, and others cut and paste.

Chapter 5—Creative Art Enhances Learning

After reading this chapter, students can develop their own topics for guided learning through art, which include other curriculum areas. Using the chart on page 108, they indicate the types of development inherent in their proposed activities.

Chapter 6—Reaching Out to Other Expressive Arts

1. Read to the group the Brooklyn Bridge project description on page 140. Have participants compile a list of experiences and activities that could expand this project, using each of the art forms: 2-dimensional and 3-dimensional art; music/sound; movement/dance; creative drama; poetry/prose. Ask participants to select a theme of interest in their community that would be appropriate for young children and to develop a broad range of experiences around that theme, incorporating all the arts. Encourage them to share their ideas with other group members.

2. A class or workshop group might listen to music that has a distinctive style or mood (for example, flowing, lyrical pieces). Using scarves or streamers, participants can capture the flow of music, and then list words which describe the action of the scarves or steamers. Each participant can use some of these words to compose descriptive phrases or a poem. Next, create sound pictures (see page 131) or a sound accompaniment for the poems. Or add creative body movement patterns to the original words and music.

Index